Alexandra Fullerton

HOW
TO
DRESS

SECRET STYLING TIPS FROM
A FASHION INSIDER

illustration by
Bijou Karman

PAVILION

LET ME SHOW YOU HOW TO DRESS

thought long and hard about the title of this book. Who am I to tell you how to get dressed? I am certainly not a paid-up member of the fashion police, nor a boob-grabbing Hooray Henrietta who wants to coerce you into curve-enhancing prints that flaunt your bangers.

I *am* a fashion editor with seventeen years of experience on magazines, and I have worked on an array of British publications including *Stylist*, *Glamour*, *Grazia* and *Stella*, along with contributions to the international editions of *Vogue* and *Harper's Bazaar*. My day job as a stylist sees me searching through the high street and designer catwalks to edit the trends that will work in reality and discovering the gems of the season that are really worth buying. On photo shoots, I have dressed all sorts of bodies from Olympic champions to the perfectly plus-sized, from tinily petite pop singers through to Amazonian models – encompassing every figure, shape and size in between. My job is to always make everyone look great. And that's empowering for me and for them.

I've appeared on radio and live panel talks to discuss and dissect everything, from the craze for clogs to seasonal trends and the state of the British high street. I am properly obsessed with clothes, shoes, bags, belts, sunglasses and jewellery, and when I'm not at work I spend my time trying on my wardrobe, working out combinations of clothes for different occasions and playing with new outfits or shopping, whether that's for me, a client or the window variety.

I promise you, I know my stuff when it comes to getting dressed.

The definition of 'how' is 'in what manner, by what means', and my aim with this book is to show you the ways and means with which you can dress well. I want you to use this book as a guide. It's a set of ideas, a collection of formulas, a gathering of stylish tips and fashionable principles that will give you the guidance to build outfits that work, that won't look 'off', out of proportion or weird. By the end you should feel excited about getting dressed, you shouldn't ever wail, 'I have nothing to wear!' and you will know how to make the most of the clothes you already own with the secret styling tips I've shared. Best of all, knowing how to dress means that people will focus on you and not your clothes. For want of a better analogy, this is a recipe book that encourages you to use your own ingredients and follow the recipes within to mix up the perfect outfit.

When people find out what I do, they always ask what they should be wearing this season, what the colour of the moment is, what new things they should buy. But getting dressed well is so much more than buying something in, say, pillar-box red just because it's 'in'. I want this book to celebrate your personal style and not be a bible for following fashion. The processes I go through at the start of each season echo the way you would approach getting dressed and going shopping, and that's how I've decided to set out the chapters in this book. You will start by thinking about what you'd like to wear, how that fits with your lifestyle, what you might need to buy and how to deal with actually making a purchase. Then we'll move on to how you should store your clothes when you get them home and all the little ways to make an outfit come alive.

I start by explaining style and fashion. The two concepts are very different and although they are often lumped together, acknowledging that they are not the same is absolutely crucial and the first thing to learn in your dressing journey. You can skip chapter one if you already know the difference between fashion and style, although it's not a long chapter.

Working out your own signature style comes next, and I share the ways in which you can explore your sense of self through your clothes. This is how to edit yourself. Once you've discovered your own personal style – whatever it may be – you'll still need some fail-safe items you can turn to in a crisis.

Chapter three could be a standalone read. Essentially, this is a shopping list of all the pieces you need to own to build looks that work consistently well. Like houses, outfits need solid foundations. That doesn't necessarily mean sturdy bras and knickers, but key pieces you can build the rest of a look on.

Once you've acknowledged what your own style is and realized what you need in your wardrobe, it's time to go shopping. It's not enough to pick something up from a rail and hand over your credit card at the checkout. Chapter four is a coaching exercise in building a proper shopping strategy, whether you are shopping online, actually on the high street or in the mall. The goal is to ensure that you aren't lured by the sales or spangly items that you'll never wear. If you are searching for more practical advice, the middle chapters, How to Shop and Your Wardrobe, are the pragmatic ones. When you get your new buys home, you need to present them properly to get the most out of them, and I have some tips on dealing with wardrobe detoxes, too!

Finally comes all the expert, insider knowledge I've gathered during my career. These are the secrets to styling yourself like a fashion pro. Skip straight to chapter six if you want to know the way to roll your sleeves and be let in on the formula for the magical Third Piece.

This book isn't a hard-and-fast set of rules; after all, as chapter seven advises, fashion should be fun. I want you to fall in love with getting dressed as much as I do and, armed with a few new ways in which to do it, go and get dressed in whatever you want.

FASHION

VS

STYLE

FASHION VS STYLE

No one has said it better than Yves Saint Laurent: 'Fashions fade, style is eternal.'

But if it really was that simple to navigate dressing well I wouldn't be writing this book, and the biannual merry-go-round of catwalk shows would be obsolete. In essence, fashion is fast and fashion is fun. At its most powerful, fashion can be an important reflection of our time and society. Whoever thinks clothes are irrelevant beyond covering our modesty and keeping us warm has no grasp on the power of fashion to express your politics, desires and tastes. Fashion can be cruel – it's whimsical and fickle – but if you learn how to play it to your advantage you will feel on top of the world. Style, meanwhile, doesn't care about what's in or out. Style does its own thing. Style knows what suits it and isn't averse to breaking the rules. Style is the person you want to hang out with. Everyone has a girl crush on style.

Truly stylish outfits will stand the test of time and look as chic, elegant and engaging in decades to come as they do right now. Looking at photos of outfits that are fashionable means you will be able to date them exactly, down to the season or month as well as the year. Fashions are ever-evolving and incredibly fashionable pieces that you wore to death for one month will look tired and dull the next. Items that are stylish will last until you wear holes in them. Although fashion and style may sometimes be interchangeable, 'fashion passes, style remains.' I think of this Coco Chanel quote often, not least when I break down each season's new

Start by looking at
your body in underwear.
What shape are you?
What clothing silhouettes
suit you?
They're the ones you get the
most compliments from and
feel the most confident in.

trends. At the moment, the fashion industry is caught on a treadmill of presenting new styles ever more speedily to tempt shoppers with ever shorter attention spans to hand over the money they might otherwise spend on cinema trips, holidays and special meals. The fashion system, and how we shop, is changing, which is why it's now particularly pertinent to explore the differences between fashion and style.

WHAT WORKS FOR YOU

Even though fashion won't last forever, that doesn't mean you should dismiss its place in your wardrobe. There is a tightrope to be walked between dressing so stylishly that your look becomes dull, and looking current. Some people argue that foregoing fashion in favour of style equates to being boring. Not true. One of the aims of this book is to help you look stylish *and* fashionable, if you want to, without looking like a fashion victim. If you can grasp the difference between style and fashion, then far be it for me to dictate what you should and shouldn't wear, but I would like to present a fail-safe guide that will help you get dressed, the tips and formulas that will save you time, as well as explaining why certain pieces go together. These are the general rules that will help you to look good and feel even better, and dressing stylishly is a perfect starting point. Style is often about paring things back and relying on good-quality basics.

There are many old-fashioned 'figure fixes' around, but who wants to wear halter-necks all the time just because they have a pear-shaped rear? (And needing your 'figure' to be 'fixed' is such a hideous concept.) You should appraise your shape honestly and keep in mind anything you're particularly proud of, or perhaps want to keep under wraps, and then be reassured that by following the rules of proportion, almost nothing will be out of bounds when it comes to getting dressed.

If all your clothes were confiscated, where would you begin a re-stocking shopping trip? What pieces would you want to return to? Even if you pick jeans and a T-shirt, upgrading these pieces from basic to becoming stylish means adding little twists of personality that come from your own likes and dislikes as well as your personality. What style and shape of jeans and cut of T-shirt would you pick? How would you wear them? Jane Birkin became a style icon for her reliance on jeans and a T-shirt. But if you analyze her look further, it was always a skinny fit, scoop-neck cap-sleeve T-shirt worn with high-waist, flat-fronted wide-leg jeans. She'd wear flat shoes or sandals and always carry a basket. Princess Diana was a denim icon of the 1990s and favoured a tapered silhouette and stone-washed shade, but she'd wear her denims belted high on the waist with a double-breasted blazer and loafers or ballet flats to make them feel smarter and less hippyish than Birkin did. You can see that both women – although thirty years apart – had echoes of current fashion in their outfits, so they didn't look out of place at the time, but were still ultimately timeless. These clues are visible in the wash and cut of their jeans and what they chose to wear them with – and, of course, their hair and make-up. Their basics looked relevant to the era but were also stylish because of the styling each woman applied to her outfit. Style is about personal choice: how you roll your sleeves, the type of shoes you choose. Starting to bring style into your wardrobe, if you've previously been overwhelmed by following fashion or perhaps didn't care for style at all, means playing it safe to start with. If you don't know yourself and your style yet, don't take risks. Keep it simple and pared back. After all, some of the most stylish women of the last century were known for style that didn't shout.

THE EVOLUTION OF STYLE

As we settle into a new century, it could be argued that, perhaps inevitably, all the great style icons lie behind us. The momentous changes that society went through in the twentieth century gave birth to dozens of style tribes, each with their own distinctive look. Much of the time they were forced into existence by music and political sub-cultural movements, but what is there to be part of these days? Will hipsters, normcore and grime become as sartorially relevant as teddy boys, hippies or punks were in another fifty years' time? Today, people have many more ways of expressing themselves than just through their clothes. What looks will appear on the mood boards of fashion designers of the future? The truly great designers of the last century – Coco Chanel, Cristobal Balenciaga, Christian Dior, Yves Saint Laurent, and even Calvin Klein and Donna Karan – recognized that the way women dressed formed part of their emerging social roles, and reflected society as a whole through the clothes they created during their most successful periods. Designers now produce garments to get the most likes on Instagram.

Nothing is more damaging to creativity than nostalgia, but if you're looking to find great examples of style, it's likely that the women who are cited as the most stylish all lived in the previous century. What follows is a list of ten of the most stylish women ever, although there are of course many others. These are the women whose looks have stood the test of time, and who have become a byword for dressing with flair, often thanks to their appropriation of one particular signature piece. And while the appearance of many of these women on the world's best-dressed lists will come as no surprise, thanks to their classicism and polite elegance, I have included some less predictable picks to show that rule-breakers can be as stylish and inspiring as their more minimally minded sisters.

THE CLASSICISTS

BRIGITTE BARDOT

The ultimate French *ingénue*, known as much for her love of gingham as her heavy pout. Bardot's 1960s outfits – which majored on capri pants and off-the-shoulder tops – have become shorthand for insouciant French Riviera chic, and feature in shops and on catwalks every summer. 2017's runaway trend for having your shoulders on show saw all such pieces described as 'Bardot'. Having an item named after you immediately bestows style-icon status. #Goals.

AUDREY HEPBURN

Many of the characters Hepburn played have their own inimitable style – Holly Golightly's little black dress and long gloves in *Breakfast at Tiffany's* and Princess Ann's full skirt and neckerchief in *Roman Holiday* – yet Hepburn's own style is equally recognizable. Gamine, simple and perfectly elegant, she knew how great she looked in a black polo neck and wore one on repeat, which makes her look totally relevant today, too.

FRIDA KAHLO

With outfits as rich in colour and detail as her highly surreal paintings, Kahlo provided a masterclass in mixing print and pattern and clashing colours. The traditional details of Mexican costume that she co-opted also show how hidden symbolism in your clothes can reveal your ambitions, and Kahlo used the origins of her favourite pieces to weave a story that hinted at myths, gender and femininity. In an era when society didn't have access to a constant social media narrative stream, Kahlo's clothes show the power that can be had through letting one's clothes speak volumes without having to say a word.

JACKIE KENNEDY ONASSIS

Brigitte may have had the Bardot top, but Jackie O had sunglasses (oversized, slightly square, extra dark) *and* skirt suits (neat, boxy, straight-cut in pastel bouclé tweed). With the budget of a first lady turned wife of a shipping magnate (and with a Wall Street-banker father and socialite mother) some may argue that her style was bought, but Jackie's perennially simple and immaculately put together outfits made elegance her number-one style priority, and that certainly isn't a shoppable commodity.

JANE BIRKIN

Hermès named their iconic Birkin bag after the British singer and actress, despite the fact she was known for carrying simple straw baskets, and Jane is the best example of how good style can bestow even the most casual pieces with extra panache. With the right choice of belt and simple shoe, Birkin elevated the essentials, and although she looked totally of-the-moment during the 1960s she still provides style inspiration today. Not least to Alexa Chung, three-time winner of a British Fashion Award, who admits, 'I've just been ripping off Jane Birkin.' Me too. Jane is the ultimate example of dressing to suit your lifestyle as well as tastes.

THE RULE-BREAKERS

DEBBIE HARRY

Not all style icons are demure and elegant. Seventies singer Debbie Harry feminized purposefully angry punk styles by adding plenty of sex appeal. Harry shrunk the shapes of tomboy denim, added saucy cutaway details to dresses, chose tight-fit silhouettes wherever possible, picked provocative slogan tees and brought ripped and frayed edges to the masses. Today's generic rock-chick look – and Kate Moss's signature style – would be unimaginable without Harry's trailblazing style having gone before them.

KATHARINE HEPBURN

Hepburn wore menswear before androgyny was fashionable, and proves that style comes from knowing your own mind. The classic pieces she chose – white shirts, tailored trousers, Oxford shoes – became innately 'hers' in the styling. Shirt collars were always popped and were tucked neatly into extra-high-waist, wide-leg trousers (known as Oxford bags.) At the time, her appropriation of men's clothes was audacious and daring, proving that true style sometimes involves taking risks.

GRACE JONES

Jamaican-born Jones is also unafraid to break new ground with her style choices. As we move through the decades our collective vision becomes far harder to shock, but Jones' collaborations with the fashion and art world's most daring creatives have seen her style become much imitated. From her sharp-suited androgyny, penchant for bondage-

inspired leather, body-conscious silhouettes, statement jewels and ever-present hoods, Grace Jones is fierce, and proves that being brave with your style choices will take you far.

IRIS APFEL

Only coming to prominence as a nonagenarian, interior designer Apfel has a signature style that could politely be referred to as eclectic. Her goldfish-bowl round glasses, arms full of bangles and fists full of rings are proof that you don't need to remove one thing before you leave the house in order to be stylish. Take that, Coco! Stylishness seems to ricochet from the pared back and simple to the wildly bold, and Iris is the epitome of the eccentric end of the spectrum. Colour, print, texture, jewels upon jewels upon jewels, Apfel wears them all brilliantly.

MARCHESA LUISA CASATI

With regular appearances on designers' mood boards – she provided inspiration for Alexander McQueen and John Galliano during his tenure at Dior – this Italian heiress and one-time richest woman in Italy was a patron of the arts. Although wearing live snakes as jewellery, which Casati famously did, is not to be advised, her devotion to style remains as important a lesson today as during her lifetime. While living in exile in London she was spotted searching through bins for feathers to decorate her hair, and was buried in leopard print. True dedication to style.

What all these women demonstrate is that great style is often found either by paring down one's look to a simple uniform, or by breaking so many rules that the traditional laws of good taste no longer apply. Perhaps, at this point in history, there is no room for future style icons to be born, especially if we believe that there's no such thing as a new idea. Will Kate Middleton ever surpass Princess Diana's formal elegance? Will Beyoncé or Rihanna be referenced as ground-breaking musical style icons in thirty years' time? Kim Kardashian's almost blind allegiance to fashion is commendable, however unflattering or ridiculous she may look, and even Lady Gaga's meat dress was inspired by the artwork of Linder Sterling in the early Eighties. Future style icons would do well to consider the style heritage that precedes them to help them find a unique voice in the melee. We will watch this space.

FAST FASHION

One other discussion worth having on the subject of style versus fashion is the growing anti-fast-fashion movement. Sometimes, when I wander around the flagship stores of the cheaper brands, I wonder *who is going to buy all this stuff?* And where will it all end up? At the time of writing, 235 million items of clothing are expected to clog up the UK's landfill sites during the year, and as prices drop it's not difficult to see the correlation between cheap clothes and the value we place upon them. If you buy a top that costs the same as a couple of large coffees, which will only get a few wears before boredom sets in and the seams start to fray, chucking it in the bin seems a reasonable course of action. The many steps that have to be taken to produce it, though, from harvesting the cotton to realization and transportation, are surely worth more than a few quid. Handing over a sizeable chunk of your hard-earned wage packet will hurt, but the payoff will likely be an exquisite piece that will keep its value and stay in good shape long into the future.

But sometimes we all need a quick fix, and the high street does a very good job of presenting us with myriad on-trend options, although some trend prediction experts are predicting the demise of fashion trends as we know them. Fashion is notoriously cyclical and it doesn't take a genius to work out that if one summer brights are in, next year it's likely to be a dark season. Likewise, designers tend to have two ways of tackling their inspirations. They either move on drastically from what they currently do, ricocheting from short hemlines to long, for example, or make a gradual move away from this season's motifs. The biggest shift in recent years is the acknowledgement that brands have a USP and that as consumers we are happier to be affiliated with certain labels than we are trends. Shopping only for trends is a fickle and unfashionable way of approaching your wardrobe. It's also the least stylish way to build personal style. A far more authentic approach is to pick shops that echo your own taste and buy fewer pieces that will last you longer.

THE SIMPLE LIFE

With all this in mind, if you want to dress stylishly, keep in mind that restraint is key. It's always better to be underdressed than overdressed. The most common reason that fashion stylists say they dress minimally and utilize a plain uniform when dressing themselves is to save money. If they didn't stick to a simple style they would be bankrupt from succumbing to all the pretty things that cross their paths. But there are plenty of ways to bring out your fashion personality without wearing monastic garb.

Whenever you want to add something new to your wardrobe, try to follow this five-step plan for successful shopping that won't cost the earth:

1 Buy from ethical brands that follow a sustainable business plan.

2 Look for vintage or second-hand items to avoid being part of the quest for constant newness.

3 Make sure your purchase is made to last, constructed from quality materials.

4 Only shop if you absolutely have to and make sure you love, and will wear, your new buy.

5 Look after and love your existing pieces, repairing them and cleaning them carefully where necessary.

Each season, navigate the trends with great care. Make sure that, if you bring highly fashionable pieces into your wardrobe, they work for your lifestyle *and* your own look to ensure they are more than a one-season wonder. The truly brave will ignore all the trends (but where is the fun in that?), so make sure that you really love a piece before you buy it. If purple is the colour of the season, buy a belt or a pair of shoes in the shade. If oversized sleeves are the silhouette *du jour*, experiment by getting a grey marl sweatshirt that includes the detail so you will feel like you are casually acknowledging the trend; it will be far easier to wear than a silky evening dress with balloon sleeves. And never forget your personal style, which we will move on to in the next chapter. Iris Apfel doesn't wear bracelets *and* brights because she thinks they look good. They *do* look good, but she wears them because of the colour and the stories attached to her collection of bangles. What can you bring to a simple outfit that will change it up and make it yours? Is Elvis your musical icon? Could double denim be your signature style? Will you never be seen in jeans? Have you a collection of pendants you could wear every day? Find a theme you can adopt and incorporate it into your outfits to give them a jolt of personality.

SIGNATURE STYLE

SIGNATURE STYLE

n the fashion world we are bombarded with what seems like a trend a minute. So many clothes, so little time. It can be overwhelming when you come face to face with a fashion cupboard crammed with rack upon rack of the most extravagant and exciting new pieces of the season. There is always a temptation to revel in variety and try on everything, all at once. But the mark of the truly stylish is restraint, even if a bird of paradise is your spirit animal. You don't have to live by Coco Chanel's advice to take one thing off before you leave the house, but you'll see that some of the most stylish women in the fashion industry stick resolutely to a uniform approach to dressing themselves. Whether they choose brightly coloured tailoring, sporty jackets, vintage prints or an armful of bangles, it will be a look that they don't stray far from, whatever the trends of the season dictate. Adopting a signature style doesn't mean you have to abandon the chance to have fun with fashion and play with seasonal trends, but it will make your overall look far more coherent and ensure that the clothes you have in your wardrobe work harder together and look more smoothly styled.

What you wear, and your signature look, should be as much a part of your DNA as the fact that, for example, you hate coriander, read Russian poetry to relax and have a crush on Tom Hardy. These are the best methods to develop your own signature style.

THE MAGIC WORDS

The first step to getting dressed is knowing who you are. It's not what you want to portray with your clothes, or who you'd like to become in five years time – it's far simpler than that. Just acknowledge and make peace with your life, your current lifestyle, your body, your likes and dislikes and be totally truthful. Look back through old photos. What did you feel most comfortable wearing? Which outfits give you the happiest memories? What do you wear again and again when style inspiration (or your alarm clock) fails you? Which piece got you the most compliments? Your answers will give you clues to the items that should form the building blocks of a brilliantly edited wardrobe that will always feel like *you* and never let you down, whatever, whenever and wherever you have to dress for.

When you look into your closet, the ultimate goal – and what I want this book to help you to achieve – is to find an array of options that all go together, that *all* fit and will *all* make you look and feel fantastic. When you have begun to unravel and acknowledge your personal style, you'll move on to the fun task of editing your clothes and ensuring that you never fling open your bulging wardrobe doors and cry out that you have nothing to wear.

There's a quick trick to building an edited selection of clothes you can always rely on: you simply choose three words that describe your style. And by style, I mean how you actually dress day-to-day, which pieces in your wardrobe get the most wear, where you go and what you do. This is not fantasy fashion; it's not what you would splurge on if you won the lottery. Take into account your lifestyle, your favourite pieces and your style icons... there should be three words that totally sum up your style.

To get you started, my three words are:

SIXTIES DENIM TOMBOY

And I promise that everything in my wardrobe ticks off this combined description. I'd never sway towards anything too feminine (I just feel prissy), a Seventies silhouette (too hippy for my mod state of mind) or patterns (for me, denim is the perfect base that goes with everything else in my wardrobe). I can run around in pretty much everything I buy and if it looks as though I could have swiped it from my husband's wardrobe, all the better (that's the tomboy element). With these three words you can exactly envision what my style is, what my key pieces could be, what goes with what and how my outfits pan out.

Now, what are yours?

ANDROGYNOUS

TWEED

FEMININE

PLAYFUL

GRUNGY

SPORTY

FLAMBOYANT

LUXURIOUS

SEXY

RUFFLES

PREPPY

MODEST

SILK

GIRLY

ROMANTIC

VINTAGE

SLICK

A-LINE

WIDE-LEG

ECLECTIC

PUNK

TRADITIONAL

ELEGANT

MINIMAL

DETAILED

CLASSIC

SIMPLE

PARED-BACK

TONAL

TIGHT FIT

HIPPY

COLOURFUL

HAND-CRAFTED

Your three words may be none of these things, but the list is designed to get you thinking about what your style is. Once you've settled on three words, everything you buy from now on should fit the mould, and anything in your wardrobe that doesn't sit within those parameters should go the way of the charity shop. You might find yourself wandering round Topshop chanting your words under your breath like a mantra as you hold up potential buys, but it will make shopping a million times less expensive and wasteful.

Sometimes (confession: actually quite often) I'll fall in love with a top, trousers, dress or skirt. The fabric, the price, the life I'd lead in it... I keep coming back to it, circling it, dreaming of it. But whatever it is, I always leave it on the rail if it doesn't fit with my three words. I know it's not me. It will just sit untouched in my wardrobe, or I'll brave an outfit with it and end up feeling at best uncomfortable or at worse ridiculous. And that's the difference between developing a wardrobe that makes getting dressed a joy and ending up with a closet full of beautiful things that don't work together or just don't feel right. So much of what we wear comes down to the physical feeling of clothes on our skin. Comfort, whether psychologically or literally, is key, and building an edited wardrobe will ensure that feeling remains.

BREAK THE RULES

However many rules (or rather guidelines) I suggest in this book, one of the most important is to feel free to break them. You'll see that the truly stylish woman knows her own mind enough to understand when she can skip the black-tie dress code, or that colours that clash can really go. Playing around with fashion 'don'ts' shows that you have confidence and a fashion ability that will give you true style. I was once told I had perfect taste but, although it was meant as a compliment, I think there is something a little more exciting about outfits that have an element of bad taste or a flash of the weird in them. Some of my favourite ways to rip up the fashion rule-book follow here.

1 Never mix navy and black

It's actually the chicest colour combination going, but a perpetual 'don't'. Maria Grazia Chiuri, creative director at Christian Dior, dedicated a whole collection to this 'off' mix for autumn 2017 and it looked phenomenal: chic and mysterious. What other odd colour combinations go together? Mauve and emerald; orange and sky blue; mustard and shocking pink... have fun putting unexpected shades together. As a guide, colours that are opposite each other or next to each other on the colour wheel have a natural affinity. Also, look for shades that have a similar intensity. A soft, washed-out brown could look odd against a strong, zingy blue. The only shades I would steer clear of wearing together are red and green. They go brilliantly with each other because they're both bold, but they also make you look like an extra from *Elf*, and that's not really a fashionable goal. Recently there has been a trend for tonal dressing, or wearing one colour from head to toe. This is an eye-catching way to dress, but can be overwhelming. If you're going for one colour all over, I suggest mixing the tones so you have an array of shades in your outfit. Try wearing an array of reds ranging from merlot and raspberry through to scarlet, and always mix up the textures to give extra interest to a one-tone look. A fake fur jacket worn over a woollen polo-neck and velvet skirt, perhaps with a patent handbag and canvas sneakers, would help stop a monochrome outfit feeling overpowering.

2 Never mix gold and silver

Traditionally this is a jewellery no-no, but I think the tones look beautiful if they are artfully combined in a stack of bangles up your arm or coiled around your neck. Add rose gold, blackened silver, brass, copper and more. This sort of rule-breaking will add an element of bohemian style to any outfit and is a definite 'do.'

3 Dress appropriately for your age

When there are clothes on sale for toddlers that seem more suitable for strippers, and the Duchess of Cambridge wears clothes that have a lot in common with her step-mother-in-law's wardrobe, it's difficult to know what 'age appropriate' dressing is any more. When I buy things I always try to visualize myself wearing them when I'm in my sixties and beyond. I am in my late thirties and I want to buy clothes that have longevity to them. I also know that I might feel bad about my knees or upper arms in twenty years time, but just because I'll have reached a half-century by then I won't want to throw away all my mini-skirts. I plan on wearing them with thick tights and just mixing up the layers of coverage so I can still get joy from my favourite pieces for many years to come.

4 Don't mix your prints

This is a style trick you will need to take a little bit of time to work out because it can be awkward, but clashing prints definitely *can* be worn together to fantastic effect. The key is finding two prints with a similar base shade; a good neutral will make it easy. And then mix up a large, bold design with a smaller, more delicate pattern to give your outfit a twist. Two small, ditsy prints will

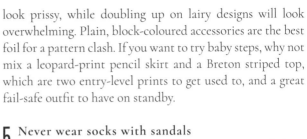

look prissy, while doubling up on lairy designs will look overwhelming. Plain, block-coloured accessories are the best foil for a pattern clash. If you want to try baby steps, why not mix a leopard-print pencil skirt and a Breton striped top, which are two entry-level prints to get used to, and a great fail-safe outfit to have on standby.

5 Never wear socks with sandals

You only have to take one look at former *Vogue* fashion director Lucinda Chambers and know that this is the most ridiculous rule of all. The combination beloved of English seaside boarding-house residents (complete with knotted hanky on their head) became a favourite styling motif on the catwalks of Prada and Marni. A chunky 'Dad' sock and a sturdy sandal such as Birkenstock's Arizona or a velcro Teva, are the best combination. But a jazzy lurex sock and a fancy strappy party sandal look just as creative. This one-time 'no' works because it subverts the norm (which would be bare feet and sandals) in such a bold and unexpected way.

6 You can only wear shorts on the beach

(See also: *you can only wear trainers in the gym.*)

Making the most out of your wardrobe involves thinking creatively around some items. This outdated rule was created because styling shorts in a holiday-ish way, and teaming your trainers with sports kit, is the obvious way to wear them, but think beyond this and there's a whole array of outfits you can make. Your shorts could work with a chunky sweater, opaque tights, biker boots and a leather jacket in mid-winter, while the trainers would add a frisson of edge to a silky maxi dress at night. Your dress code is only limited by your imagination and you can wear whatever you like, wherever and *when*ever you like!

BE INSPIRED

Now you know that finding yourself (from a fashion point of view) and breaking the rules are starting points to developing your own personal style, you need to bring something to every outfit that only you do and stick to it. I always wear denim, and never put together an outfit without one element of it in, even if it's a pair of shoes or a cuff made from a length of ripped up jeans. Caroline Issa, fashion director of *Tank* magazine and a favourite of street-style photographers, is known for wearing immaculate tailoring, often in jewel-bright colours. Anna Wintour, editor-in-chief of US *Vogue*, is hardly ever spotted without a pair of skin-toned peep-toe Manolo Blahnik sandals. When your friends are out shopping, the highest compliment is for them to see something they think you'll love and send you a picture. If they get it right, you know that you've nailed a signature style.

At the international fashion shows, while there are trends emerging on the catwalk, I also get tons of inspiration from seeing what the other attendees wear. Which way do they tie a scarf, how do they stack their rings, how do their trousers fall, what colours and textures and fabrics do they mix… Start to do the same with people you know and meet. Get analytical. If you like their look, think about why it works and what part of it you are attracted to. Is it the bright patterns, the lack of jewellery, the fancy shoes? These are all elements you can incorporate into your personal style. Next time you're catching a train or a plane, watch the people waiting. People who dress alike will imperceptibly gravitate towards each other along the platform. Your vibe attracts your tribe and the way you dress is a way of speaking volumes about yourself without even opening your mouth. Start following fashion accounts that attract you on Instagram or build a Pinterest board of people whose style you like. To start you off on your style stalk, some of my favourite fashion insiders are Jo Ellison, Donna Wallace, Christene Barberich, Ruth Chapman, Natalie Massenet, Tamu McPherson, J J Martin and Phoebe Philo. These women all have an authenticity to their outfits which, however disparate their looks might be, is the consistent thread that I want to take and recreate in my own outfits. What you find in yours may well be very different: it could be colour, it could be playfulness, it could be a collection of brilliant mohair sweaters. But just starting to look at other stylish people will help you to develop your own style. For more on this, see pages 22–25 and 152–3.

PROPORTION

Whatever pieces you choose to include in your wardrobe, the way you wear them is key. My pet hate – and the thing that ruins your outfits far faster than spilling tomato pasta sauce down a white shirt – is not considering proportion. As well as matching up the perfect pieces, spend time looking at the lengths and shapes of your clothes (and how they work together) before you leave the house. However chic your separates might be, if you put them together in a combination that knocks your body shape out of proportion, your outfit will fail. There are so many times that you envision an outfit but it absolutely does not work on the body (this is why dressing up and practising your outfits in front of a full length mirror is crucial). A few key points to remember with some of the trickiest items follow.

COATS

Your skirt or dress should never peek out more than a centimetre (half-inch) from under your coat. There have been so many times I've wanted to stop people on the street to advise them that the hemline is *all wrong*. Having several inches flap out from below your coat looks sloppy and makes your overall shape look wonky. It will also make your legs look disproportionately short. There's nothing wrong with short legs, but when your body looks as though it's too big to be supported by your pins, which is what this mismatch in lengths will look like, you should worry. There are exceptions, of course: for example, if your coat hits your knee and your skirt is a fishtail style that flares out from knee to mid-calf, this silhouette would work. Also, if you are wearing a full ball-skirt length, a mid-calf trench will work because the entire leg will be covered. But these are very specific exceptions, so it's safer to play by the style rules on this occasion and make sure the coat and skirt finish at the same length. If your coat is mid-calf and your skirt is mini-length, this will also look wrong because the amount of leg on show will throw the look off balance. Team knee-length with knee-length, mini with mini and mid-calf with mid-calf and you can't go wrong.

MID-CALF SKIRTS

These can be tricky, as this modest shape has a rather matronly whiff about it. There is a major trend for elegant pleated versions at the moment and they look great with a chunky heel or a sturdy flat shoe, but make sure that the fabric of your skirt is light. What works best for all shoe scenarios with this length skirt is a semi-fitted top. A shirt that skims your top half or a neat sweater is ideal. You can definitely wear a chunky oversized knit, so don't think you have to stick to the old rule that you must wear one loose piece and one fitted one; soft, billowing chiffon pleats with a slouchy woolly sweater looks great. However, I would advise a heeled shoe with this voluminous combination to elevate your outfit and stop you looking like you're about to drown in too much fabric. It's a very glib fashion solution – 'darling, just add heels' – but the height and elongation that even a small heel gives your ankles is priceless, and sometimes your shoes are just the right thing to evaluate when you're stuck with an outfit that's almost, but not quite, right.

MINI SKIRTS

By its very nature a short skirt will show off your legs, but you didn't buy this book to be told the blooming obvious. As well as the proportion in your clothes, it's important to consider the proportion of skin on show with an item. I think you can go as short as you feel comfortable in (opaque tights will be a modesty life-line) but for the rest of your look, choose pieces that balance out the lack of length in your skirt. Starting with the shoes, an open-toed strappy sandal can feel out of kilter with a mini, so I would choose an ankle boot. The extra coverage over your instep will balance out bare legs. The heel can be as high as you like. This advice isn't about dialling down sex appeal; I love over-the-knee boots with mini skirts, but what is key is balancing out the ratio of skin and silhouette in any one outfit to keep your overall look in proportion. Any type of flat, from an Oxford to a ballet

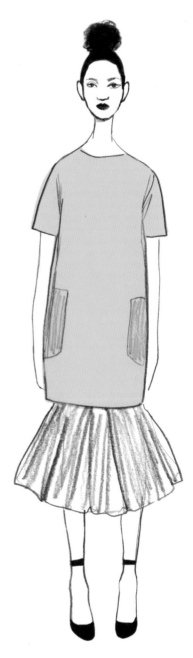

slipper or a gladiator sandal to a flip-flop, will work with a mini. If you're wearing your short skirt on holiday, then a loose man's style vest looks great with this length, as does a semi-fitted shirt or a chunky sweater, if you're not heading to the beach. Unless your skirt is A-line or wider in volume, I think fitted blazers look too insignificant with this skirt length. Your top half needs to be grounded by a bit more volume, so a double-breasted pea coat or high-necked Aran knit will be the best balancing act.

VOLUME

Don't be scared of trying out super-sized shapes. They bring strength and edginess to your outfits, and with a little consideration make a clever statement about style. Just continue to think about elements that could throw your outfit out of kilter. It does depend on where the volume lies in each piece. A pair of palazzo pants and a super-chunky sweater are two voluminous pieces together. If you add stilettos, it could look wrong (like you're about to tip over) so a chunky shoe, whether heeled or flat, will work best. Try plain-soled trainers like Adidas Stan Smiths. A floor-length maxi-skirt in heavy wool may look like it's swamping you, so the key is to find a bias cut or fluted shape, rather than A-line, if you want to choose such length. If the fabric is light, silk or chiffon, a spindly heel could be the perfect balance for this type of skirt, as a flat could, visually, look too hefty. A full skirt, in the style of Dior's New Look, is voluminous and also works with spindly heels. It would look 'off' with flats, but if you want to be a little more creative with your outfit, this could be a good thing. Those in search of an intellectual take on the voluminous trend should look at Japanese designer Rei Kawakubo's designs for her label Commes Des Garçons. Consistently taking the 'right' and making it wrong, Kawakubo plays with silhouettes and volume in an eccentric and exciting way.

As you discover what proportions work best, keep in mind that clothes conspire to play tricks on the eye and can make a perfectly innocent outfit look awful on the body, via optical illusion. You just need to have a few crafty tricks up your sleeve to outwit the outfit.

One final shortcut to style? Wear trousers that are the right length for your shoes. Always hem your trousers to go with heels *or* flats to make sure that the trousers just graze the top of your shoes and are no further than a couple of centimetres (half an inch) from the floor.

ESSENTIAL ITEMS

THE
ESSENTIAL
ITEMS

Sometimes, in the dead of night, your clothes couple up and breed. A few extra pieces creep into your closet, you find yourself utilizing The Chair for storage and a floordrobe starts to spread menacingly across your bedroom. It's a scene worthy of a bloodcurdling Hammer Horror scream. But this isn't a movie. It's real life, and what's twice as terrifying is finding yourself in the middle of the mess with the clock ticking and NOTHING TO WEAR. At times, I have been guilty of thinking my wardrobe was made from elastic, so swiftly did I stuff it with new things there really wasn't room for, let alone the need for. The point of this book is to make getting dressed a far easier process than it is now. If you follow these guidelines and ensure you always have these essential items in your closet, you will take a giant leap towards that goal.

THE 10 ESSENTIAL ITEMS EVERY WOMAN SHOULD OWN

Editing your wardrobe is essential to make your morning routine as smooth as possible and to eliminate any tricky decisions about what to wear. Building a capsule wardrobe around these ten trans-seasonal pieces will mean you are covered with a solution for every occasion. Choosing a tonal palette, where the colours of all the pieces work with everything else, is key, as is memorizing the formula of what goes with what. These pieces *can* be tweaked to accommodate your personal style. Perhaps you're just not a trouser person, so you should replace this piece. But the goal of this capsule wardrobe is to make a variety of outfits that all work together instantly and let your brain get on with other things. Disclaimer: you will need a few seasonal updates, such as a warm coat for winter, plus another sweater. Maybe add a leather trouser. When it gets warmer, bring in a light cotton bohemian summer dress plus of a couple of camisoles or vests. If you go out *a lot*, perhaps you will need an evening dress. You can't survive on ten pieces alone, despite what some style bloggers profess. However, for the majority of the year these are the items you will turn to again and again for the refreshing ease with which they go together, and they will *all* alleviate morning wardrobe rage. Guaranteed.

1 The biker jacket

It's the shortcut to ultimate cool. The leather Perfecto-style jacket (as named by American brand Schott and first manufactured in 1928) is the last word in versatile outerwear. Worn by Marlon Brando in *The Wild One*, The Ramones and every rock star worth their riffs, it will make a ball gown look modern and give your downtime outfits streetwise style. Right now, embellished, embroidered and slogan-smeared styles are having an on-trend moment, but I recommend investing in a classic leather style – in navy, black, dark chocolate or khaki – and you'll be covered for every eventuality.

2 The denim dress

A personal favourite, I have about thirty denim dresses in my wardrobe and it's become my signature piece. But even without my overt dedication to denim (and I admit, I have an addiction) you need a denim dress in your wardrobe. Layered over a T-shirt it looks relaxed at the weekend, and when sharpened up with a blazer, bold belt and a handbag that means business, it brings an unexpected edge to your working wardrobe. My favourite styles have a sixties, A-line silhouette that are easy to layer. Denim shirt dresses are particularly versatile, but steer clear of floor-sweeping maxi versions that can look a little too festival-ready, unless you are actually heading to Coachella.

3 Good jeans

Ignore whatever's in fashion, whether it's spray-on skinnies or the recent craze for cropped boot-cuts. Your perfect jeans should flatter *you* and fit your lifestyle. I've found that boyfriend styles suit most body shapes and look perennially cool. But work out what your most flattering fit is and stick to it. Choose a mid- to high-waisted style for longevity and pick a pair that finishes above the ankle, whether hemmed or when rolled. This will give the most versatility when you're choosing your shoes and will let you work a heel, flat or trainer. Darker denim shades are always smarter and can take you through to evening with more dash than a snow-washed ripped pair. Paler washes always look more casual, even when they are pristine, and they are certainly more summery. Your perfect jeans can even do double duty as dressed-down workwear if you choose immaculately pressed indigo and team them with a blazer or reworked shirt.

4 The sweater

A sweater that you can throw over T-shirts is a layering must and, as knitwear goes, will always be more useful than a cardigan. The vagaries of fashion have thrown logo sweatshirts, cut-away shoulders and embellished cashmere into the style spotlight recently, but as you are building a capsule wardrobe that you can wear to infinity, classic should be your watchword. A crew neck with full-length sleeves and ribbed cuffs and collar is the ultimate buy. Bigger busts don't necessarily need a V-neck style to flatter as long as the knit isn't too heavy. Pick a colour that will lift your mood *and* go with every other item in your wardrobe. Cobalt blue, rust or emerald green are shades that are one step away from being a neutral but give your look a little boost. Choose wisely and you can wear this piece with jeans at the weekend, at night with a statement skirt or to the office with tailored trousers.

5 The statement skirt

This is the piece I rely on when I need to make an entrance or do the straight-out-from-work dash. It always feels special and considered but isn't as flashy as a 'going-out' top or cocktail dress. Depending on your personal style, a laser-cut leather mini, brocade midi or lace pencil will work best. Mixing something fancy like this skirt and something casual (try a T-shirt) is the ultimate in High–Low dressing (see page 109) and every stylist's secret method for looking pulled together without trying too hard, which is also my personal style nightmare.

6 Polished trousers

When I want to look chic, my black Balenciaga cigarette pants (found on eBay for £18) are the only answer. They work hard as a professional saviour with shirts and blazers, as well as looking elegant after dark with the sparkle of costume jewellery and a half-unbuttoned silk blouse, inspired by Helmut Lang's iconic images of Yves Saint Laurent's tuxedoes in the 1970s. Choose a slim-fitting pair for the most long-lasting style. Wide legs will date faster than a fit that skims your body, and cuts that stop above the ankle are the ultimate in flattering silhouettes. This will also give you the freedom to choose any shoe shape instead of worrying about excess fabric draping on the floor, which is *so* not chic.

7 **The T-shirt**
Where would we be without the humble T-shirt? The classic gender-free cotton cover-up only came to prominence in the free-thinking 1960s – before then it was considered underwear – but the T-shirt's sheer versatility means it wins a place in our capsule wardrobe. Choose V-neck or crew, as suits your body shape, and pick a neutral colour that will both enhance and counterbalance your other choices in this edit. I particularly like wearing my gauzy linen T-shirts under a blazer with jeans, inspired by French *Vogue* Editor Emmanuelle Alt, or with a statement skirt as a surprising take on the eveningwear dilemma (with a little extra sparkle from my jewellery box!).

8 The 18-hour dress

Once you've found the one, it will change your life. This is the dress that you can throw on without a thought at 6 a.m. before dashing out the door for a day of school runs, coffee runs and supermarket runs. With just a change of shoes and perhaps an earring swap, the right 18-hour dress will take you through cocktails, dinner and even dancing. This dress should almost be a blank canvas, as you will need it to be ultra-versatile. Some of my favourites include a khaki twill, cap-sleeve knee-length version from Zara with drawstring ties at the waist, and a black broderie anglaise shift from Warehouse.

9 The blazer

Far more effective than a cloak of invisibility, slipping on a perfectly tailored blazer will give you infinite power and polish. Psychologically, I always feel more pulled together in sharp tailoring and even if your jacket isn't bespoke (whose is?) you can fake it incredibly easily. High-end designer pieces are always impeccably cut but err on the small side. Taking a high-street jacket to have the sleeves nipped in is an affordable shortcut to demi-couture style. Double-breasted designs are having a moment thanks to Alexa Chung's seal of style approval, but a single-breasted blazer will be eternally chic. Find a style with slim, detailed lapels in satin or leather and mix with contrasting colour bottoms – never the same shade – or it will look like you're wearing a split-up suit.

10 Reworked shirt

Crisp and clean, a shirt is the ultimate hardworking piece. Tucked into sharp cigarette pants and worn with point-toe stilettos, you mean business; untucked over jeans with bare feet, it's a Calvin Klein perfume campaign on the weekend; pop the collar, add chandelier earrings and a ball skirt and you've got an individual way to do black tie. Designers have been creating clever ways to transform the classic button-down and give it extra edge (look to Palmer // Harding, Monographie and In Grid for the most intriguing versions). Your shirt should go with every item in this capsule wardrobe (even the dresses, if they are layerable) so while there are a huge array of belts, cut-outs and lengths to choose from, keep the styling relatively simple. I would always choose white to get the most mileage from this piece.

REPEAT BUYS

When I chat to friends and colleagues about how they shop, they roll their eyes and complain that they end up with a dozen of the same-style item – and nothing that goes with them. I am also guilty of the repeat buy. My weaknesses are leather mini skirts, denim dresses, long-sleeve, high-neck lace tops (my default evening option, with jeans) and flat point-toe shoes. Even Carine Roitfeld, global fashion director of *Harper's Bazaar,* has admitted to the odd repeat purchase – black pencil skirts are her thing. There is absolutely nothing wrong with knowing your figure, accepting your style and revelling in it by buying a few versions of the same thing; there will be seasonal updates that will make your choice of classic feel fresh, and as long as you balance out your wardrobe with enough other pieces that go with your signature piece, there is no shame in being a repeat offender. If all your navy pea coats get equal wear, you're doing all right. Do try to rotate your repeat purchases. Sometimes I have fallen into a repeat-buy pattern to try to replicate the perfection of one item, but none of the new buys live up to the first and I just keep on wearing the original. That isn't repeat buying, it's just madness.

ESSENTIAL ACCESSORIES

In the same way as it makes sense to categorize your clothes into the key pieces you will turn to again and again, it's also true of the finishing touches to your outfit: the accessories. These are the styles you should build a capsule accessory wardrobe from, and that will cover absolutely every occasion. If you want to add more, stick to these essential shapes and styles to grow a useful collection.

SHOES

1 The classic court
This is the shoe that means business. For meetings, interviews, after dark or to add an edge to your jeans there is something incredibly empowering about wearing your highest heels. Search for an elegant shape with a pointed toe – although avoid exaggerated and elongated toe shapes, as they make your feet look extra-long. The softer the angle, the more flattering they will look. Pointed toes are more timeless than round toes, which do cycle back into fashion every few years; but if you're looking for longevity, Manolo Blahnik's BB style is the ultimate power stiletto. With a flattering toe shape that flashes a little toe cleavage and a slim stiletto heel, this shoe will really work with every skirt shape or trouser in your wardrobe.

2 The mannish flat
When you want to look smart but need to be fast, an elegant menswear-inspired flat is the perfect solution. Based on an Oxford or Brogue style, lace-up or with monk straps (those that buckle across the instep of your shoe) this shoe is strong and stable. Like the classic court, it will be versatile enough to go with almost everything in your wardrobe. Perhaps only a narrow pencil skirt that ends mid-calf will look wrong with this shoe shape, dependent on your height. I particularly love the look of them with a slim-leg trouser suit, and seek out classic brands such as Church's for timeless styles.

3 The sneaker

Down-time dressing calls for something more relaxed. The canvas Converse All Star or Adidas Stan Smith in white leather will have the ease of a trainer but are pleasingly minimalist, so will work as a shoe substitute, too. Try your sneakers with sharp tailoring or an ultra-feminine party dress to work the High–Low mix (more on this on page 109). The only caveat is that these are not shoes you would actually play sport in, so any style you would consider wearing to do more than run for the bus in can't be considered as one of your essential six shoes for style.

4 The mid-heel ankle boot

For sheer versatility, the ankle boot wins its place in our top six shoe styles. The knee-high boot and thigh-high versions are brilliant styles and if you're venturing out into the cold nothing beats an over-the-knee for keeping you warm, but I promise you will get the most wear from a boot that hits no more than 5 cm (2 inches) above your ankle bone. Any higher and it will start to get into that unflattering mid-calf zone, any lower and it will become a shoe-boot, which are really awkward to wear any type of trousers with. Choose a boot that has a 5–7-cm (2–3-inch) heel because they will go with most outfits. If you're not keen on wearing high heels, don't panic. As it's a boot, your foot will be held in place and will feel more secure than it would in the same height heel in a mule or open sandal. Keep an eye on how the boot sits around your ankle and choose a style that fits closely. Too wide and it could look a little bit wellie-ish. Ankle boots always have a slightly punky feel to them, so you can go one further and choose a style with studs (like Givenchy's iconic studded flats) or straps, but remember that they need to stay fairly unadorned to work with everything in your wardrobe. Acne's Pistol boot is a classic in this category.

5 The party heel

This is the shoe you can have fun with. For evenings when you're going all out *and* out out, you want to have a shoe that looks like it's going to have as much of a good time as you are – although the party heel will look as good with your smart tailored work trousers and jeans as it will with a posh frock. Look at what you're most likely to wear with them. Are you all about the LBD? In that case, a colourful jewel-toned satin will be a perfect contrast. Do you like your jewels to make the statement? Search for one-tone, block-colour styles. I have specified a heel in this category because nothing feels more party-appropriate than slipping into heels, although I am also a huge fan of the embellished evening flat, which will add an insouciant glamour to any outfit. Dune consistently do amazing styles in brocade and satin with diamanté details that will elevate any after-dark look.

6 The summer sandal

With the addition of a flat, easy-to-wear, warm-weather sandal, your essential shoe wardrobe will be complete. This style should be simple. Search for something that looks like it's been made by generations of artisans overlooking the Mediterranean. In fact, two of the best sandal brands – Ancient Greek Sandals and K Jacques – have. Tan leather gets better with age, but if you're wearing your sandals in the city, and perhaps need to wear them in the office, a darker tone will be smarter. Gladiator styles are a summer perma-trend but have been overtaken by the simple slide in fashionability terms. Keep them unadorned for authenticity – it looks wrong to see a basic sandal smothered in crystals – and if you have long ankle straps tie them around your ankle only. Straps snaking up the leg might work on Greek goddesses, but in real life you will look ridiculous and spend all day trying to keep them in place!

BAGS

Being a self-confessed shoe addict, I couldn't limit myself to any less than six styles, and since shoes have to be practical (you need to be able to walk in them) you need more choice. Bags are a more straight-forward proposition, however: they need to carry different amounts of stuff. The end. Although I have dozens of bags, the foundation styles you need to base your bag collection remain the same, and are as follows.

1 The carry-on tote

Some days you just need a little more *stuff*. A roomy tote made from hard-working leather is the smart choice. This is decidedly *not* a shabby cotton bag to put your lunchbox, spare trainers and laptop in. This bag is sharp and sizeable. It will also be the perfect accompaniment to a smaller bag – in a tonal shade – if you need to double up on your accessories. If you choose a large enough style it works brilliantly as a carry-on bag when you're travelling, so look for styles that come with ready-made organizational pouches to help simplify your life. I have a brilliant version from Mon Purse, which can be customized to your colour specifications.

2 The cross-body satchel

Depending on the finish and colour you choose, this is the ultimate weekend option, and also works brilliantly when you're in town running errands. The cross-body strap makes it a little more casual in feel, and should allow you to carry the essentials and go hands-free. Cambridge Satchel's original school-style bags have become modern classics, and thanks to their structured shape they are still smart enough to wear for work and on the occasions when you need to be a little more polished. In this category, leather styles are still my choice over canvas, as these will tip the style into scruffy territory with just a few wears.

3 The after-dark clutch

The smallest item in your essential bag arsenal. Like the party heel, this accessory should be fun, witty, bright and glamorous and make enough of a statement to start conversations. Olympia Le Tan creates the cleverest little clutch bags based on vintage book jackets, although I like to spend less on a party bag, in case it gets sticky with Champagne or smeared with canapés (truly the mark of a good night out), so try Accessorize in the UK for the widest high-street selection. When you're shopping for this sort of bag, pack everything you are likely to need into a sealed sandwich bag and try it out with the bags on the shop floor. If they're in a sandwich bag you won't leave something in the clutch accidentally, and the slippery plastic will make it easy to swirl your belongings around inside it.

4 The structured shoulder bag

For when you are travelling light, but aren't as relaxed as the cross-body requires, this is what you need. An elegant dark tone that will look smart for years, one little outside pocket for quick access to a travel card or lip balm, a shoulder strap and perhaps a top handle. If you need to look polished and chic at any time, pick a smart shape that keeps itself together. Nothing beats Chanel's classic 2.55 if you have a rather large windfall to spend, but the Balenciaga City bag is a less expensive investment (and it comes with a mirror).

EVERYTHING ELSE

If you're making a style statement with an outfit, the accessories you choose are the perfect punctuation to your look. For each of the categories below, I've listed the key styles to consider. Choose what works for your personal style and lifestyle, and you'll be all set.

Jewellery

What you wear close to your skin is so personal; jewellery holds memories and sentiments that are beyond the vagaries of fashion. I am a minimalist when it comes to extra adornment – I don't even have my ears pierced and only wear my engagement ring on special occasions – but I do have a collection of jewellery that I turn to when the mood strikes and I need to give my outfit a little extra lift.

My essentials are: crystal costume necklaces (that look like you found them in your grandma's jewellery box) for slinging over a grey marl T-shirt and jeans. Chandelier earrings to wear with swept-up hair and backless dresses after dark. Cocktail rings that look like boiled sweets – add one or two per hand on a night out. Tiny diamond rings and narrow bands you can stack and that will bring subtle sparkle to dull days. Pins and brooches that will add life to your basic denim jackets and plain knitwear. Delicate chain necklaces and tiny pendants you can layer over bare skin and strappy summer sundresses. Acrylic and beaten metal cuffs – I like stacking a couple on each wrist for symmetrical style.

Sunglasses

The number-one rule here is to shop for what suits you. For years, I was obsessed with aviators. I wanted to be an aviator-wearer so badly until I realized that they made me look cross-eyed. Be guided by your face shape alone. There are certain guidelines: square faces suit rounder frames, round faces look better in square shapes, sharp features can carry light, wire-framed styles and heart-shaped faces are balanced by cat's-eye designs. But nothing beats having a huge try-on session in a department store, where there will be myriad brands and shapes to try. Take a load of selfies and note down the style of every pair of sunglasses you like. Make sure any contenders fit you properly – nothing is worse than spending a day pushing your sunglasses up your nose or removing a pair of shades to find deep indents on the side of your nose. When you know what suits you, you can return to a similar style. Even supermodels have sunglasses that suit them best – and some that don't work with their faces – so there's no need to build up a collection of sunglasses in every style. If you want a new-season update, search out new colours or frame details rather than choosing an on-trend silhouette that might not suit you.

Belts

I could put a belt on almost every outfit I wear or style. Even a wedding dress looks better with a ribbon sash! Belts will add a finishing touch to any outfit, however plain, and are as essential as shoes to creating a look. You should certainly start building up a bank of belts that will add magic to your day-to-day outfits. Start with a wide, beaten-leather style that you can thread through jeans. Add a dark leather or patent style that will look perfect with a city-smart shift dress or cigarette pants, then add a narrow version, too. A wide corset-style belt in leather or canvas looks great over crisp shirting and is a current fashion favourite for an edgier, trend-led option, and a fancy fabric belt that you can wear at night with velvet trousers or over a lace dress will complete your capsule collection. Add more finishes – such as mock-croc, satin, brocade and studded – as you can find them, and you will soon be converted to never going out without a belt.

Hats

Widely acknowledged by the fashion pack as a shortcut method to getting noticed by street-style photographers, hats are quite literally the finishing touch to any outfit. The mood of your look can be totally transformed by your headpiece, but the essential styles are:

1 The baseball cap
Sporty and street, snap-back caps have had a resurgence as a fashion item thanks to backing by labels such as Balenciaga and Vetements. A leather cap looks particularly slick, while a clever slogan will add extra edge. Wear your baseball cap with a tailored jacket and high heels (*never* a tracksuit) to juxtapose the laid-back mood when you want to be a total fashion badass.

2 The beanie
A cold-weather essential with more than a hint of grunge about it. Soft mohair knits look great with biker jackets and floaty floral skirts. This is the weekend essential when you plan to go on long walks through the mist.

3 The fisherman's cap
A naval style with a sharp peak, this cap feels totally 1960s and therefore goes brilliantly with skinny ribbed knits, vinyl mini skirts and pea coats. The structure makes it smarter and, although it's a semi-casual weekend style, it works for bohemian city escapades, too.

4 The fedora
Not to be confused with a trilby, which has a narrower brim, true fedoras have a deep inset at the crown, and deeper pinch creases at the front. This smart style has a retro tinge, so keep the rest of your outfit modern.

Trench coats and skirt suits will make you look like a gangster film extra, but rough-edged denim or chunky tweeds will work well.

Scarves

What scarf you choose, and how you tie it, says a huge amount about your style. This section has nothing to do with the weather (although classic woollen scarves with tassels are essential for bundling up in the cold) and is all about elegant silk scarves that work year round. If you feel your outfit needs a little extra oomph, a slip of silk could be just what you need. Long, narrow ribbons of silk feel rock-inspired; a neat little cravat tied around your neck is dainty and prim; a low-knotted printed scarf looks preppy; a bandana tied bib-style under a western shirt looks cowboy cool... and, as well as the dozen ways you can wear a scarf around your neck, don't forget that these versatile accessories can be used as headscarves, belts, bag handles and even tops if you learn to tie them the right way.

The game-changers and hero pieces

Now that you have all the essential pieces hanging and folded in your closet ready to wear, you should find getting ready every morning a cinch. But each season there will be a slew of new items begging to win a place in your wardrobe and waiting to update your basics. This is the fun part, where a well-chosen high-street gem or designer investment piece will give your everyday outfits a lift and make them feel fresh, on-trend and seasonally appropriate. By only choosing things that work with your personal style, and that you're certain you can already team with three other items in your wardrobe, you should be able to ensure you'll get plenty of wear out of them, and perhaps elevate them to hero status.

HOW

TO

SHOP

HOW TO SHOP

While Britain used to be described as a nation of shopkeepers, I think calling us a nation of shoppers would be far more accurate. When I was growing up, the weekend wasn't worthy of a Monday-morning watercooler catch-up unless you'd spent half of your free time trawling up and down the shopping centres of the land looking for a new top to wear on Saturday night or a posh frock for a smart Sunday do. Everyone seemed to know exactly how to navigate the offerings in store, and could target their favourite shops with ease. For me, going shopping was my default treat if I had done well in an exam or was celebrating a birthday – and I wasn't the only one.

But a lot has changed.

The Noughties saw a British shopping landscape revolutionized by amazing overseas imports, when previously the choice had been limited to perhaps a dozen stores. Pre-Zara, pre-Cos, pre-Mango, the UK had the best high street in the world, but what we now have is even more incredible. Whatever your style, you'll find something for your price point, body shape and occasion. But too much choice can be paralyzing. When you open your closet to decide what to wear, you'll find the decision far easier when less is more. A 20-page menu of pizza toppings is just going to terrify you, and 20 buzzing shops to trawl through in the quest to find one winter coat is equally frightening.

As well as the sheer amount of shops to visit, our lives have changed and we're not as well practised at shopping as in yesteryear. Instead of hanging around in fitting rooms, friends now spend time brunching, gallery hopping or taking a spin class together, then going for green juices post-workout. Our increased need for experiential activities to fill our hard-earned leisure time means that looking at clothes in shops has slipped way down the weekend to-do list. Time is precious and however many Prosecco bars, live DJs and chill-out zones the shops put on for us, it's just not enough to entice us back to the high street in the volumes we once visited.

The actual retail experience leaves much to be desired, too. Service is negligible, bordering on completely absent. If you don't take the right size into the changing room, you'd better be ready to put your clothes back on and traipse onto the shop floor for a rummage. Asking for alternatives from the stock room will result in eyes rolling and you'll be delving into piles of unfolded clothes to find that elusive 'L' length for hours. I overheard one shop worker on Oxford Street advising a half-dressed shopper behind the fitting room curtain that it would be a 20-minute wait before someone could even begin to look for the requested size. The collective attitude on the part of shoppers seems to be that if you can't be bothered to help us, we can't be bothered to shop.

Of course there are many diligent store assistants who work hard to help shoppers choose clothes that suit them, fit them and make the retail experience a smooth and joyous one again, but the consensus from my friends is that they'd rather poke their eyes out with a credit card than visit a high-street chain store. Big shops are the ones that carry the most inviting stock, but they're turning into fashionable supermarkets (yes, they even have self-scan tills now).

Shopping should be fun, a displacement activity, something we do for the pleasure of it as well as an end in itself. It shouldn't be a chore, but neither should it be as much of an adrenaline rush as playing poker. You've seen the figures; footfall in our stores is suffering, yet we are all still buying clothes like nobody's business. Online shopping is exploding and new brands are breaking through at a rate of knots. Fast fashion is speeding up but I believe we've forgotten how to actually shop IRL (in real life) – or perhaps we haven't all undergone the rigorous training and research that shopping-obsessed me has. To begin to tackle real-life shops successfully, you need a strategy.

SHOPPING STRATEGY IRL

There is a way to successfully navigate the high street and actually enjoy the experience, or at least come away with some purchases that you're going to wear. That should be the goal but, as with every sport, preparation is key before you hit the shops.

1 Make a list

Just as it's foolhardy to head to the supermarket aisles on an empty stomach, or text your ex after necking three Old Fashioneds in an hour, you should never rock up to the high street, credit card in hand, looking for a life-changing pick-me-up purchase. You'll have the most success when your mood is shopping-neutral. There are times when you just fancy a browse and feel in need of an injection of something fresh into your wardrobe – but guys, it's *dangerous* out there if you're searching aimlessly. You could find a cute little skirt or a fling-worthy frock, but it will likely be just the fashion equivalent of junk food. At best you'll feel hungry again in an hour, at worse you'll be left with stinging remorse for weeks. It's far less reckless to have analyzed your wardrobe and decided what you really need to make your outfits work (or what you really want to freshen up your closet for the new season), then shop with a purpose. Before you even make a list, you should define your style (we did that in chapter three) so that you're ready for the next step. If you're serious about adding a new fashion element to your seasonal outfits, you need to spend some time browsing your favourite magazines to give you an idea of what those key pieces for the season will be. When you come across a reworked shirt, cold-shoulder sweatshirt or high–low hemline, you'll recognize their newness (at the time) and be able to pounce.

2 Timing is everything

When you shop has major impact on how successful you will be. You should look forward to a shopping trip. If you head into the high street resenting the fact you have to shop for a dress for your second cousins' second wedding and give yourself an unrealistically short timeframe, you'll walk straight into problems. So make sure you can devote a proper chunk of your diary to a shopping expedition. You should always shop at a time when you feel relaxed and can hand over those couple of hours, guilt and commitment free, to concentrate on fulfilling your shopping goal. Knowing what you will be up against is essential. You need to stay relaxed, so heading out on Saturday afternoon isn't going to help you keep your cool, as this is the busiest time in stores. Browsing on a Monday morning will, though. Scope out your favourite stores: befriend a sales assistant, ask when their biggest deliveries take place and visit the shop when you know there'll be fresh goodies to discover. Mark those days in your diary, and whenever you spot something in a magazine that you want, if it's not online already, call up and get a drop date. Diarize everything, and you will be rewarded. As well as the physical timing of your shopping trip, think of when is best for you mentally, too. If you leave work at 6 p.m., hungry and eager to get your feet up in front of a box-set, visiting the shops won't be a happy replacement activity. If you clock off buzzing and eager to go out, redirect your energies to the shops instead of the pub but be aware that post-5 p.m. is a busy time in shops. When you work out a time that's right for you, shopping will be so much easier.

3 Use your phone
We are totally blessed with the capabilities of the smart phone when it comes to working out a strategy for successful shopping. A seasonal flick through the glossy magazines and a mental wishlist would once have sufficed, but now we can screen-grab, pin, note-take and mood-board to our hearts content. Use your phone at every opportunity when you're preparing to hit the shops. Start by categorizing your wardrobe and working out exactly what you're shopping for. Take pictures of the pieces you already have in your wardrobe to remind you of what your new buys need to go with or the gaps you are due to fill. Make a folder of street-style, pictures of women who wear the intended item with inspired style or screenshot editorials from Instagram that showcase those items in outfits and highlight your must-buy pieces. Take plenty of selfies of you wearing similar styles that you already own or whenever you're wearing a colour that particularly suits you. These will be an aide-memoire to avoid any misguided impulsive purchases in purple when you're looking for an immaculate white shirt. When you're in store, show pictures of what you're looking for to the sales assistants; they might have just the thing out the back. I always do a lap of the store and snap any items I'm keen on as I go round. You might love the tweed coat hanging near the door but prefer the one near the till. Taking pictures saves you from carrying everything around the store while you umm and ahh, and lets you edit what you want to try on before heading to the fitting room.

4 Dress up
A shopping trip was always a special occasion. Growing up, I'd dress up in my fanciest gear and use at least three eyeshadows before darkening the doors of my local high street. Now, time has compressed my shopping trips

into less leisurely affairs but they are still super fun, whether I'm doing essential market research, stockpiling basics or adding a few new treats to my wardrobe. And although I don't dress as though I'm going-out out, I still like to put together a shopping outfit. The better you look, the better your shopping experience will be, from the treatment you'll receive from the shop assistants to the way you see yourself when you're trying on your potential haul. Unless you like to go *au naturel*, wear make-up and get your hair into some semblance of array. You'll be spending your time gazing into mirrors so you don't want to be distracted by a face that could look better glaring back at you. For me, many a shopping trip has been abandoned because I just looked too rough to face a mirror.

Wear as few layers as you can get away with for the season. Shops are icy in summer while air-con blasts but coming into a store from the rain-lashed street in winter will leave you sweltering. Make sure your outfit offers easy-to-move-in comfort and is easy to peel off and put back on, but don't be too scruffy or, weirdly, you might find your mood won't let you take the shopping trip seriously. Dress like an off-duty model: soft jersey round-neck tees (no fiddly buttons), a canvas shacket (a hybrid shirt/jacket that you can throw on or tie round your waist if necessary); and your preference of trouser or jeans. Add some fancy shoes that you can walk

in – Gucci's cult Princetown backless loafer has the ultimate mix of comfort and glamour – plus the smallest cross-body bag you can manage. This will leave your hands free for browsing.

Think about what you'll be potentially trying on. If you want fancy strappy sandals, black socks that leave lint all over your toes might make you feel awkward. If you need a new bikini, don't wear a pair of pants bigger than the bikini bottoms you're looking for, and if you're after posh frocks or going-out tops, slip on a neutral, strapless seam-free bra so you can envisage what your new purchase needs underwear-wise. Buying a dress that you'll never wear because you don't have the right underwear should be banned. Trousers need the correct heel height to make them look right, but that means carting round an extra pair of shoes all day. That would cancel out my rule of travelling lightly, and you'll want to wear your new trews with more than one shoe, so I would advise you do a rudimentary try-on to ascertain waist and hip fit, then work out the nuances of leg length at home with your entire shoe collection.

5 Spend more money

I'm not encouraging you to be frivolous. I'm certainly not inciting spendaholic behaviour. I'd simply like to reveal that there is a part of your brain that reacts in the same way as if you were feeling pain when you spend a significant amount of money. If you find an amazing charity shop bargain for pennies, you won't flinch. Buying three jersey tops for a tenner won't even register on the pain receptor. 'A lot' of money means different things to different people, but if there's no pang of pain in your brain, there's no emotional connection when you shop, and it's far easier to simply wear the item once, then leave it to landfill. A lot of money is spent in fast-fashion chains that have questionable morals when it comes to treating their factory staff and seem to use less environmentally friendly methods of production. The fast-fashion system is the subject for a whole other book, but if you can stretch to a financially bigger purchase that makes you wince, makes you think, makes you really work out whether you need it and will make you wear it more in the long run, it has to be better for you, the fashion industry and potentially the planet.

SHOPPING STRATEGY IN VIRTUAL REALITY

Now you know how to navigate the madness of the high street, online shopping should not be the fallback option. Many of the same rules should be adopted when shopping from the comfort of your own home or your phone, but shopping virtually needs as much of a strategy to make it successfully to the Pay Now button as if you were standing in a queue. This is how you should shop online for the happiest outcome.

1 Toughen up

You need to approach online shopping with a steely determination to only buy what you came for, so making a list is something you should certainly take from the IRL shopping strategy. You're shopping because you have a gap to fill for a certain something. Don't deviate. There's a constant temptation to pop 'just one more thing' into your basket to qualify for free shipping or the misguided reasoning that if you're getting the dress anyway, you might as well add a top. It also seems so much easier to walk away from a till in person than a full basket online. The music was too loud, you got bored waiting, you were hungry... however much I've desperately wanted to buy something (and this includes phenomenal sales bargains and killer 'It' items) if the energy and mood aren't right, I can walk straight out the door. Online stores will often save your basket for you for months, so even if you come to your senses about the sequin T-shirt you loved on Monday morning it will still be waiting for you while you browse online on a Thursday night, wine glass in hand, perhaps. (Important: most online purchases occur after 6 p.m.) The feeling that shopping online is not like spending actual money is real, but train your brain to stick to buying only what you need. Before you buy, make sure you've checked the delivery and returns policies. Never choose the most expensive

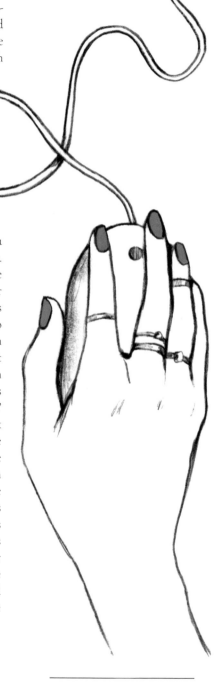

delivery option and only buy if you're offered free returns. If you've spent a significant amount on getting the item delivered in the first place – and it costs the same again to send it back – there's a huge temptation to keep it and let it languish in your wardrobe. And however much you browse, never actually buy anything when you've had that glass of wine.

2 Be an editor

The way that websites are merchandised can be just as tempting as a store layout, which entices you to spend by showing you exactly what items go with what. Colour co-ordinated sections presenting all a brand's product will help you visualize some great trousers to go with that jacket (add to basket) a belt you simply must have (add to basket) and as soon as you click on an item you like, you can see it styled up into a whole new look you're just one page away from replicating (add shoes, bag and shirt to basket). Hone in on what you need: go straight to the category you're shopping for and stay there. Use the filter options with abandon. I like to browse what's new on asos. com every day (it's my one weakness) but I'm only interested in their own-brand product. On multi-brand sites, select just the labels you want to wear. You're busy. Choose your sizes (add one up or down, if you really want to) to avoid the agony of finding that one perfect piece that isn't available in your size, especially on outlet sites or at sale time. Filter out colours that don't go with anything else in your wardrobe, cut out silhouettes and lengths that don't suit you and ignore prices you shouldn't be spending. You could lose days in the bottomless rabbit-hole of online shopping, so bring the principles of editing a shoot rail to your online shopping strategy. Videos are always helpful as they reveal any little design details, such as cutaways or splits, that you might not notice on a static model.

3 Make time

Set an hour aside to simply scroll. Just as you would plan a real-life shopping excursion with no interruptions, you'll need to give over enough time to ensure you can have a clear online shopping session. While you could browse, break for supper, mull over your options, then go back and buy, jumping up to feed the cat, make a phone call or hang out the laundry during your allocated shopping time won't be conducive to making successful choices. Online makes it so much faster to buy and lets you have an incredibly easy retail experience. You can have half a dozen windows of your favourite sites open and flick between them, comparing and contrasting the pros and cons of each lurex sweater before making a decision. If you're on the high street, you would need to be in a department store or a mall that offers a personal shopping service to have such an array of choice in front of you, otherwise you'd be popping in and out of the shops like a cuckoo in a clock. You will need to do a little more homework than you would if you were buying in store, though. Because you're losing the sense of touch, check out the fabric composition and zoom in on the detail shots to get a proper sense of the weight and feel of the item you're buying. Because online stock tends to come from a central warehouse, if it's sold out online it's usually sold out in store too, whereas if it's sold out in one store there's a glimmer of hope you may still be able to buy it online. In the same way that I head into a store and do a speedy once-over, do the same online. Learn the days that your favourite sites put new stock up online and check them out religiously.

4 The try-on
This is the aspect where shopping online trounces the analogue shopping experience. You can get everything delivered to your house, you don't have to carry bags up and down the high street, hunt for a parking space, battle public transport, deal with mirrors that give even the most confident of women a dose of body dysmorphia from their lairy lighting and distorting mirrors, or even speak to another person if you so wish. Do give yourself a decent amount of time to try on your new buys before you make a decision. If they arrive on a Monday night but you're rushed and tired, save your show-and-tell session until the weekend to give your purchases a fair chance to make it into the hallowed halls of your wardrobe. Before you even rip off the packaging (never cut off the tags!) pull out all the possible combinations you're envisioning you'll wear with your new top/jacket/sweater. Lay out the underwear, shoes, coats, anything and everything you are likely to team with the newbie to make sure you can put together outfits quickly and smoothly. The gift of trying on things at home means you never forget that you don't have the right bra to wear under that top. Ensure the new piece goes with at least three things that you already own. And then take the tags off.

5 Know your place
Knowing which pieces to buy on the high street and what you should get online will make your experience of both types of shopping super-easy. Always bulk buy swimwear online. Your own bedroom is the best place to try it on and whatever you don't keep will be easy to take to the post office because it's light. Conversely, coats are something that it's better to buy in person. Certainly do your research online, hone in on The One, and then do a final try-on in store. Although they will be delivered to your door, if a coat doesn't fit, or you don't like the quality, you will still have to traipse

it back to return, and bulky parcels are likely to get left until it's too late to get your money back. I'm fine with buying shoes online if you repeat-buy the same brands, although some people swear that they never get the right sizes. Bags are definitely better bought from the comfort of your own home. Swapping over all the handbag essentials in a store can get messy. You *need* to check a new bag fits your keys, iPad, diary, bottle of water, umbrella, purse – but I'd rather do that on the sofa, not in full view of passing shoppers and sales assistants. Never make an online purchase unless you can see the item photographed on a person. Even if they are on a willowy six-foot model, it will give you a better idea of proportion, show any hidden layers, and reveal how it might move. Always check out shoes and bags this way too, if you can. Bag measurements mean nothing unless you can see how the proportions will look against a body.

WHAT TO BUY WHERE

You know how you're going to tackle the shops, but deciding what to buy, and from where, is crucial to your wardrobe's longevity and life. Some things are worth spending a small fortune on, but for others it's really not worth the extra cash. Although it all depends on your lifestyle and your budget, here's a guide to what to spend money on, and where you can save.

SHOES AND SANDALS

I used to be a shoe snob. I was happy dressed in high street from head to ankles but when it came to my shoes, they just had to be designer, darling. The high street upped its game and there were many brilliant styles that were not only dead ringers for the catwalk, but also desirable in their own right. But still I couldn't quite bring myself to downgrade my shoe collection, until it clicked. Designer shoes are often made from finer leather, but what about fabric shoes? They are all created equal! Whether they're pink silk heels from Prada or Zara, they are still made from fabric and are still going to get scuffed at the same rate. It's the same for raffia, white leather and summer sandals and espadrilles. Leather shoes and boots can be treated, polished and repaired but, despite some cleaning and re-dying services, fabric shoes cannot. After a few months of wear, high-end and high-street fabric shoes will look the same. I always follow the mantra 'if they're worth wearing, they're worth repairing' and everything I buy, I buy because I love it and can imagine wearing it forever. I don't want any of my clothes, shoes or bags to wear out, but since I've had this epiphany I'm happy to spend less and proudly announce that my shoes are from Next (which do brilliant shoes, by the way).

T-SHIRTS

White T-shirts are a cornerstone of every wardrobe, and black tees are likewise an essential purchase. But even the most diligent launderer will see those crisp white tees turn to grey over the course of a season, and the inky blackness morph into a less edgy charcoal tone. So, while I am an ardent advocate of spending as much as you possibly can on your wardrobe buys, T-shirts are something it's worth saving on. Some say that the cotton and weave of a designer version is superior, the fit stays straighter, the seams won't twist, but I disagree. A cotton tee is a cotton tee and it's better to buy one or two, wear them out, recycle and then replace them because I guarantee they will lose their sparkle, however much you spend on them.

TROUSER SUITS

The thrill of slipping into an immaculately tailored trouser suit can't be beaten. It's one of the pieces I choose to wear at the international fashion shows, with a quirky T-shirt underneath, a clutch bag and Manolo Blahnik's legendary BB stilettos. The mood shift to the strong, don't-mess-with-me, ruling-the-boardroom version of yourself is incredible. You really feel invincible in a great two-piece suit. (Never fasten more than one button. They look most insouciant with jacket undone and one hand in your pocket.) Now, this does depend on how often you'll wear your trouser suit, but I would recommend finding yours on the higher end of the high street. Cos, Whistles or Finery, perhaps. The vagaries of fashion mean that trouser shapes can become dated and if a suit is something you won't wear more than a handful of times a year, in about four years time the lapels might be all wrong and the waistline out of date, so please don't invest the price of a house (unless the trouser suit is one of your signature pieces). However, you also don't want to get a cheap nylon version that will sag at the bum and go shiny at the elbows, so steer clear of anything overly synthetic. It's better to have loved and lost (to have worn your trouser suit out because it looked so great) than never to have loved at all.

COATS

Cost does not directly correlate to fabric weight and warmth. If you are buying a coat for warmth (and no, not everyone does buy a coat to keep warm), I always recommend going up a size so you can slip a cosy cardi or extra layers underneath. In the winter months your coat is the first thing that people will notice about you, so choose something that echoes your personality and overall style. In the UK we tend to hammer our outerwear – or rather the weather does this for us – and unless you rarely wear it, any coat will be looking shabby by spring and really can't be eked out for another season. The high street is brimming with options and if you're on the lookout for a new winter coat from August onwards (yes, August – more on the fashion cycle on pages 140–141), you will find something individual and exciting. Wait until January and all you'll find is bikinis. Unless you're able to buy an array of coats and can splash a few four-figure sums on your outerwear, a one-season spend on the high street will be the best option.

OCCASION WEAR

I probably spend more time than most noticing what people wear, as well as wondering what other people think about my outfits, and the time this is most noticeable is for evening wear and occasions: dinners, parties, cocktail events. These are the times when you will want to look a bit special and wear something slightly fancy, but you won't be able to help yourself thinking *I've worn that before* after just a few outings. Because the cost-per-wear ratio will be high, it's better to spend slightly less on going-out outfits. Likewise with bold prints and patterns – they'll become recognizable very quickly, so unless you want to make it your signature piece ('Oh look, Alex is in her jungle-print top again') spend less. Despite this, you should never wear something just the once. As the late, legendary New York socialite Nan Kemper said, 'You should always wear it more than once, that's how they'll know you didn't borrow it.' Or, in a more everyday analogy, that's how they'll know you didn't take it back to the store after one wear.

JEANS

This is the item that many women hate to shop for, that brings on spasms of fear, panic attacks and despair. Shopping for a new pair of jeans can be painful but jeans are also the item that can give you the biggest confidence boost, garner the most compliments and give you the best-looking bum without bothering to do squats, so jeans are definitely something you should spend more on. High-street denim can have a higher ratio of elastane to cotton, meaning it will sag and bag far faster than a pure cotton material. Searching for a specialist denim brand will also be a better move than buying from a general label. Many denim brands, especially the LA-based ones, have years of specialist knowledge and garment technology which will show in their wares and on your backside. Denim boutiques like Trilogy, Donna Ida or Selfridges' dedicated Denim Studio will have a legion of sales assistants who know their brands, their fits and can work out what is most flattering for your body shape at 30 paces. Definitely spend on denim.

HANDBAGS

Some people carry their bags preciously and protectively, like vulnerable newborn babies. I sling mine on the floor. Spend less on coloured leather and fabric, and certainly don't splurge on suede. If you wear a suede bag most days for just a few weeks it will start looking shabby pretty quickly – I know from sad experience. Fork out on dark leather bags that need to hold a lot of your life for work. Evening bags, fun clutches and holiday baskets should be bought for as little as possible. You will get the least wear out of them but they will become cherished novelties that remind you of fun times.

HOW TO SHOP THE SALES

You're going to have to be blinkered, single minded, quick witted and stick to a budget. Shopping the sales is an art form, sport, mental challenge and physical workout. Here's how to do it without spending a fortune or accumulating stacks of unworn and unwise purchases.

In essence, buying something in the sales should feel like a lucky win, like finding a bank note in a long un-used handbag. Treat sales success like a surprise bonus. Try to apply the old romantic adage of stopping looking for love and letting it find you, and then the bargains and great finds will surface. Without wishing to sound like a hippy, if the universe means for you to find an Acne leather biker jacket in your size reduced by 70 per cent, you will find it.

I always browse the sales with a vague awareness of my most-worn pieces to hand. For me, that's flat point-toe shoes, denim dresses and interesting mini skirts. Keep the three words that describe your style, along with your repeat buys, uppermost in your mind too. If you shop the sales with a wardrobe gap to fill (for example, the wide-leg trouser) you'll be unlikely to score a pair. But if you do, it will be the jackpot! So loosely scan the rails for anything that looks like something you already own. Repeat buys are fine. Then, keep an eye out for any versatile neutrals, such as grey marl, black, navy and taupe, and classics such as great white shirts, blazers or round-neck cashmere. You could add a vague awareness of new-season trends with a rough shopping list; perhaps be aware that pea coats are on-trend, vinyl is the fabric of choice and the 1970s are in style. Again. Scouring magazines for advice on the key pieces for the upcoming season will be helpful if such a gem crosses your path. But keep everything loose and vague. If you head to the sale rails with an I Must Buy mentality, you will slip up and end up with a chartreuse mesh slip dress adorned with lilac and rust corsages.

70% OFF

When I reach the sales floor I find the best way is to nonchalantly wander up to the rail, scan it with your eyes – no touching, because sometimes you'll be dragged in by a piece of slippery velvet and can't help but grab it. Then, if you find something that ticks the boxes above, dive in fast. Grab like a gannet, then continue to calmly survey the carnage. Find a quiet corner of the store and look at everything you've picked up.

SALE!

Ask yourself the following questions:

1 Is it me? Does it fit my three-word style mantra? Do you have anything that is similar at home? It's OK if you do, and repeat buys are fine; they show that you know your own style. Do a mental check to make sure you already own three things it can make an outfit with.

2 Stand at the till and ask what the returns policy is, then ask again. I've been burned by stores that don't offer refunds on sale items. Are you sure you love it? Have you asked yourself everything above, twice?

3 Would you even look at it if it wasn't reduced? Then take it to the fitting rooms. It has to fit. Seriously, you will never get it taken up, taken in or lose enough weight to fit into it.

4 Now, the crucial part. Walk away from the till. Have a wander round the store. Can you walk away from the item? What if you left it on the rail? Would your heart ache? Would your other outfits fall apart? Unlikely, but there is nothing worse than the one that got away. This is doubly pertinent during sale time. It might be the last piece. Ask yourself the questions above again, then take a deep breath and go to the till.

Clothes that you should always consider shopping for during the sales. These are the classics that will never go out of style, so they should have the longest shelf life in your wardrobe.

TRENCH COATS

WHITE SHIRTS

PEA COATS

JEANS IN YOUR PERFECT CUT

LEATHER BIKER JACKETS

TROUSER SUITS**
PARKAS

PARTY DRESSES*

NEUTRAL AND DARK-COLOURED CASHMERE

GOING-OUT TOPS*

CLASSIC ROUND-NECK T-SHIRTS

* but only in the same style as those you've bought and worn before
** and only if they work with your lifestyle

WHERE TO SHOP

In the same way that it's a style sin to wear one brand from head to toe, shopping from an array of different brands is key to cultivating great style. As I plan the outfits I am going to shoot for fashion editorials, as well as the aesthetics of a look, I always consider the brand, the availability, the price and how each look will 'read' as credits. Depending on the magazine and the brief, my goal is to have a few ultra-affordable items, some investment buys and one or two hero pieces that might require a savings plan. It's good to get a mix. Clashing high street and high end is the way that many women dress today, and it's a clever way to bring personality into your outfit.

I take this editorial approach with my clothes, too. Perhaps my top will be from an emerging designer, I'll wear high-street jeans and pick designer accessories. A classic strategy is to team high-street clothes with high-end bags and shoes; stylists do this all the time with their personal outfits and I find I get less bored with my accessories than my clothes. Spend time searching every shopping source, from vintage, craft fairs and charity shops through to the high street and Bond Street to see what you can discover.

The high street is easy to access, and if you follow the shopping strategy above you will make the overwhelming mass of product work for you. It will likely form the majority of your wardrobe; if we're talking percentages, a good 50–60 per cent will be from the high street. If your budget dictates that you can't spend much on clothes and can shop only from inexpensive brands, I suggest you keep your look as simple and pared back as possible. Synthetic fabrics will always look cheap (even if they're not), so focus on buying as many natural fibres as you can and develop a signature style that doesn't date or rely on faddy quick fixes. Think of Alexa Chung in her signature pieces: a navy sweatshirt, straight-leg jeans and ballet flats. So chic in its simplicity, yet it's a really easy outfit to replicate on the high street and one that will still look great in cheaper fabrics.

Your wardrobe will soar if you can include some new, undiscovered brands. Even a tiny 5 per cent of your wardrobe will make a difference. It's my job to discover new labels and unearth fresh talent. Keep an eye on the designers associated with Fashion East. This non-profit initiative was founded in 2000 to support emerging designers by giving them a catwalk showcase at London Fashion Week. With alumni including Jonathan Saunders, Henry Holland and Roksanda Ilinčić, the new names they showcase each season are destined for greatness. These labels will give a bold jolt to your look and bring a brilliant element of surprise to an outfit. Nothing beats introducing a brand to your circle of friends, knowing you discovered them first. Check out the winners of the British Fashion Council awards and *Vogue*'s annual fashion fund competition, awarded to names you need to know (previous winners include Christopher Kane, Erdem and Mary Katrantzou) and the NewGen mentorship scheme. On a smaller scale, Etsy is a huge source of new labels to investigate and you could visit local art colleges to see textile students' work, too. If there is anything that catches your eye, speak to the students and see if you can commission them. From something as simple as a customized T-shirt to an evening dress, it's not only a way to wear something totally unique, but also support young creatives too.

The mens' department is an open secret amongst the style set. Not only do many of the designer brands offer similar pieces to what is found in their women's collections, at approximately two-thirds of the price, you're unlikely to run into anyone else wearing the same thing *and* your outfits will have an androgynous feel that is inherently cool. Stock up on sweaters, knits and T-shirts as well as pouches to use as clutch bags, to make up the next 5 per cent of your wardrobe.

Designer shoppers always justify the price of a high-end buy with the fact that they will hold their value better than a high-street piece, if they want to resell. There have been many occasions where I've compared the fabric quality of a high-street piece with designer and *totally* understood why the price is so high, but if you want to invest in filling your closet with 20–30 per cent designer gems, you need to spend time ensuring they are going to be well-worn pieces. You will also need to lavish care and repair on the pieces, if required, to prolong their life and give you a high buy-per-wear ratio. Always try to put a rubber sole on your shoes before you wear them and give your bags, depending on the finish, a spray of waterproof protector. Put your jewellery on *after* slipping into a little lace or silk something to avoid snags, and hand wash as much as you can to avoid the yellowing that intense dry-cleaning chemicals can cause.

Whatever your personal style, the final 10 per cent of your wardrobe should be made up of vintage finds and hand-me-down heirlooms. Whether that's a fantastic cardigan your mum knitted in the 1980s or a Fendi belt you found in a seaside charity shop, second-hand buys will add magic to your wardrobe and give your outfits character and personality that is lacking when you pick something off a rail, side by side with ten other identical buys. Wear your vintage pieces casually, teaming them with basics and modern items, so they don't look like retro costumes. Perhaps a brocade jacket could be worn over a grey marl T-shirt and jeans, or an elegant shift dress could have a biker jacket slung over it. From charity shops, eBay, Etsy and vintage markets, there is great vintage to be found everywhere.

There is one last category, a growing group of labels you should keep your eye on, that aren't as expensive as designer but are less ubiquitous than high-street brands. What are known as the 'contemporary' names offer an individual style aesthetic and a fresh fashion fix without the throwaway nature of some cheaper buys. Kitri, Sezane, Maje, Sandro, Finery and Ganni are all stores – mainly online – worth investigating, and are often based outside the UK, which adds even more 'where did you get that?' cachet to your look.

Before you hand over any cash for vintage finds, always make these quick checks:

1
Look at, and smell, the armpits. Yellow sweat stains from a pre-antiperspirant era will *never* come out, and when you wear the item your body warmth will ensure any lingering odours will quickly spread round the room. Yuck.

2
Hold the piece up to the light to check for moth holes and repairs that might not be visible to the naked eye.

3
Always try it on. General standard sizes have got bigger since the last century, and the number on the label won't necessarily equate to today's sizes. Unless you can actually fit into it, or are a super-skilled seamstress, leave it behind.

YOUR

WARDROBE

YOUR W<u>A</u>RDROBE

t's all very well having a wardrobe full of key pieces, essential items and new-season updates, but it's not just the clothes you have bought and carefully chosen that will ensure you can get dressed without succumbing to wardrobe rage. The way you store your clothes, shoes and bags will have a huge impact on how easy it is to get dressed every morning. We've all succumbed to the floordrobe and I have to admit to hosting a chair piled high with once-worn sweaters at the bottom of my bed, so suggesting that you banish these merry messes from your life entirely would be ridiculous and hypocritical. What I *would* like to share in this chapter are some organizational tips the fashion professionals use: the best ways to edit your clothes, and how to make your wardrobe work for you.

GET SNAP HAPPY

The biggest panic is getting dressed with a deadline. The time when you have to be out the door in seven minutes is exactly when your fashion mojo gets up and goes. There is one fail-safe way to prepare for this clothes crisis, though, because it will befall you at the worst moment possible. Whenever you have time to play with your clothes, please do.

A dressing-up session, whether it's specifically tailored to incorporating new buys into your life, rediscovering old favourites or reminding yourself of what fits, and what doesn't, is a valuable, time-saving part of working out how to get dressed. Have fun with your clothes and – this is the essential part – take pictures. Get a full-length mirror and style yourself. How would you belt that skirt? What jewellery works with that top? Slip into the outfits that you know have worked in the past, and make up some new ones. Bring out all your tops and get a list going of which ones work with what skirts. Remember what doesn't. Train your eye to work out what suits you *and* which looks will make getting dressed a breeze on those mornings when you have a major meeting and an addiction to the snooze button.

It's best if you take the pictures of yourself in the outfit to jog your memory of the details, such as whether you rolled up your sleeves or which pieces of jewellery you added. You can crop out your head if you're playing dress up on a Sunday afternoon pre-hair wash and can't face your face (it happens!), or you could lay out the outfits in a flat-lay arrangement on the floor or the bed. This 'still-life' option is useful if you have a couple of pairs of shoes that work with a particular outfit, as it will instantly remind you of the choices. If you can plan a heeled and flat shoe option per outfit you will certainly thank yourself on those days when you need to run for the bus but also take a change of shoes for drinks after work. It's all pre-planned!

You should save all your outfit pictures on your phone to remind you of what works – make a folder for easy access – but even better, print out the snaps and stick them inside your closet. When brain fog strikes, you will be better prepared to put your clothes on and get out the door without looking as though you got dressed in the dark. You can simply open your closet, look at an outfit and replicate it. Don't be tempted to go super-organized and pop them in an album, though. If the photos aren't visible at first glance, it's unlikely that you'll flick through an album to find your perfect outfit.

OUT OF SIGHT, OUT OF MIND

After seventeen years in the fashion industry and as a lifelong fashion fan, I have amassed a huge collection of clothes. I can say it's my job to keep them because you never know what you will need for the next shoot. But unless you have the same lucky excuse I do, it's really better to keep to an edited selection. Archiving pieces is a regular occurrence for me and although I have mountains of clothes, I only keep the ones I wear regularly, or that are appropriate for the season, in my closet. If you can't instantly see something, you will forget you have it. This leads to either buying more of the same thing (grey marl T-shirts, lace blouses, leather skirts – delete as applicable). Otherwise, more panic in the wardrobe will ensue as you vaguely recall that emerald-green silk shirt that was definitely somewhere... but exactly where is anyone's guess.

So, keep the clothes that you need to wear right there, in plain sight. If you have space, try the two-closet trick: one for your current and essential items and one for occasion wear, out-of-season pieces, holiday items and coats. As you go through the year you will be able to dip into the second closet for special items that veer from your day-to-day capsule without feeling too stifled or limited by a smaller edit. A suitcase slipped under your bed or a below-bed drawer also works well if you don't have the luxury of the space to house a second closet. Buying a hand steamer will mean that anything can be pristine in moments if you do decide to pull something out of the box to wear. A hand steamer is my saviour. So much faster, less cumbersome and more forgiving than an iron – every home should have one.

HOW TO ORGANIZE YOUR CLOSET

Every closet is different and every woman's clothes and storage needs will vary, but there are a few basics that will help you keep a tidy closet. You know the golden rule already, but it's worth repeating: never, ever use wire hangers. They will poke through your clothes and leave unattractive little horned ridges sticking out of the shoulder-lines of your tops and dresses. There are brilliant super-slim flocked hangers to be had, which take up hardly any space in your wardrobe. I prefer them to wooden hangers as they have the added bonus of keeping slippery fabrics in place, and the slimmer the hanger, the more space there is for clothes! Wooden hangers, which flare out and are a little wider at the ends, will be better for winter coats as they are curved and offer better support for the shoulders of heavier fabrics.

T-shirts and knitwear should be folded and never hung. Sweaters are likely to be heavy and if they are hung up, they will tend to sag and look sorry for themselves very quickly. Try not to pile your tops too high or the bottom ones will end up irrevocably creased when it comes to wearing them. And you will also succumb to the out-of-sight principle, as it will be easier to just wear the items at the top on repeat. I like to fold my tops into squares. Lay them face down, bring the arms in on themselves and lie the sleeves vertically along the ribcage seam. Repeat on the other side, then bring the hem up to the neck and stack. They will be far easier to store this way than if you fold them lengthways (bringing shoulder to shoulder) and they won't have one major crease down the middle either.

Whatever items of clothing you store in your closet, every item should be kept like with like. So printed T-shirts, slogan T-shirts, plain black or white tees and long-sleeve tees should all be in their own happy little piles. It just makes finding what you're searching for so much simpler. Split your knits into groups, too: the super-size chunky sweaters that make an appearance in mid-winter; lighter weight cashmere; round necks; V-necks. If you can have an open shelf arrangement rather than a chest of drawers it will make seeing and accessing everything so much easier, and will mean you don't create Leaning Tower of Pisa-style piles.

On the subject of folding, I fold my jeans too. If you only have a few pairs, they could be hung from clippy hangers at the waistband, but my denim collection is pushing 90 pairs, so folding them takes up far less storage space. Categorize them by cut – boyfriend, skinny or flared styles – and then stack them in colour order. It's so pleasing to see a graduated blue ombré rainbow going from snow wash to indigo.

Since you're keeping all of the same items together, hang all your shirts together. Divide them into crisp workwear, casual weekend and denim and twill styles. Hang suits together and categorize your dresses into work, casual and evening sections. You could go one further and colour-coordinate your clothes. Do as I do with my denim, and be like those interiors fanatics who colour-code their books: your closet will be a far more appealing sight if everything hangs like a rainbow. But keep the colour-blocking within items. Skirts, for example, can graduate from black through to navy, denim and white, but it would be too confusing to colour-code *all* your clothes.

Once you have seen and have easy access to all your clothes, it will be far easier to work out what you're likely to wear and what you might need to buy. As you hang or fold each section it might become clear that you have twenty tops and only three skirts. Oops! If you have access to a double rail, where you can hang shirts and jackets above skirts, you will find it helps you to become much more streamlined in your day-to-day dressing. Since everything will be visible, it will be super-easy to choose a top that matches the bottom. As a rough rule of thumb as to what should stay, you should have two tops to go with every bottom. Being worn nearer your face, tops are more recognizable and memorable, while the bottom half of an outfit tends to be more anonymous. Of course, there are exceptions to this rule if you own a highlighter-pink lace pencil skirt and a stack of grey marl T-shirts, but try to stick to the 2:1 ratio.

Some people hang their clothes in outfits, and if you have a busy week ahead I absolutely advise this. For day to day, it might not be practical, and I advise grouping by item in the long term, but if you have space then actually pulling the pieces out of your closet will make you feel so much more ready for the days ahead. You could stick little hooks on the inside of your wardrobe doors if you don't have space to hang them outside. There are clever little sticky hooks that I use in my coat closet which don't need to be nailed or screwed in to the wood. If you can spend a couple of hours on Sunday afternoon getting ready for the week ahead, you'll be able to sink into Sunday night so much more calmly, and even allow yourself a Monday morning lie-in. When it comes to fashion month – when New York Fashion Week starts the month, followed by London, then six days in Milan and finally nine days in Paris – it's crucial to work out what you're going to wear. I used to spend a whole weekend (more, if you count the time spent ordering and shopping) planning the events I would be going to and sorting out the easy, day-to-night separates and ritually checking the weather apps to know exactly what I would wear on each day, in each city. On a less epic scale, start training yourself to think in outfits. When you think of new pieces you want to buy, you should think about the outfits you will incorporate them into. When you diarize, think about the outfits you'll wear and always plan what your outfit is going to be, rather than the individual pieces you're going to wear.

What other tools do you need for storage? I'm a real advocate of using garment bags to keep things neat in your wardrobe. Perfect for storing coats out of season and keeping suits together, they're also essential for sequinned or beaded tops that could catch and anything fragile that may be damaged easily. Lighter colour dresses that might gather dust or attract dirt should be slipped into a bag, too. Use cotton ones for breathability rather than synthetic styles. I also love using metal grid dividers that keep little piles of knits in order on my shelves. Keep your shoes in boxes wherever possible to avoid them gathering dust between wears, and stick a picture on the front of the box. A polaroid or Instax snap is ideal, or print out phone shots to help you instantly identify what's inside the box. I have been told many times to stuff unused bags with tissue paper to stop them losing their shape, but once I've filled them with stuff again I've never had this problem. I hang necklaces up on hooks so they are easily seen and use miniature clear plastic chests to lay out my rings, bangles and brooches. Using clear plastic means it's not out of sight or out of mind, and you'll quickly remember which pieces work with which outfit.

Don't forget to dust anything that is outside the wardrobe and regularly hoover inside your wardrobe, too. Without wishing to seem too obsessive, dust and lint will form tempting homes for moths and mice to camp out in, and you want to do all you can to make your wardrobe an unappealing home for them! If you're using an uncovered rail instead of a closet, beware of sunlight. I've had some beautiful pieces (Cadbury's purple velvet flares, pink sequinned Marc Jacobs cowboy boots) fall victim to the fade from being stored in sunlight. It wasn't even direct sunlight, but now I keep my dressing room blind closed and my closet doors shut to prevent any similar clothing catastrophes.

THE SEASONAL SWITCHOVER

If you live in a cool climate there are many things you will need to have access to year round. My staples are jeans, T-shirts, cashmere knits and denim dresses. However hot it's predicted our summers will be, there will always be days that are chilly and on which getting your legs and arms out will not be an option. In the same vein, there are plenty of clothes that you won't need to wear year round, because however many layers you pile on, they will still only be summer-appropriate (or winter-worthy). For the peasant tops, muslin dresses, slip-on sandals and cut-off shorts, I have separate high-summer or holiday boxes. This is where the tiny bikinis live, and if I end up taking an unexpected mid-winter holiday (it's never happened yet, but I live in hope), I know I can go to this box and pull out everything I need to wear.

In early summer, if the long-range forecast is looking hopeful, I may pull out a couple of crocheted knits from the box and swap my indigo skinny jeans for a baggier cut, with an exposed ankle and in a paler wash. These two little updates will make you feel more seasonally attuned. I also avoid wearing opaque tights from early summer until the start of autumn. However chilly the weather is, the darkness of a pair of tights looks wrong during the lighter months. I do tend to wear jeans for five weeks at the start of this period though, as it's often too chilly to slip into a skirt; I want to look right and be warm.

As well as the summer box, there is a box (actually, both are plastic crates) with my super-size knits and snuggly dresses in. These only come out in the depths of winter, along with the duvet coats I've wrapped in hanging bags and stored in a suitcase in the attic. With every purchase I make for the extreme seasons, which will only be worn a few times a year, I ensure that it is timeless. Because you will be using it so rarely, you should aim to get many years of use out of it, and it will need to justify its cost-per-wear over a longer timeframe. Trendier items are likely to be worn for a season or two and will then wear out or get tired, so buy them in mid-weight fabrics that you can wear all year round.

WEAR YOUR WHOLE WARDROBE

If you have worked out the difference between fashionable fads and your own personal style, and shop wisely, it should be easy to ensure that your closet is full of clothes you will actually wear. But you may need a little extra help with a few pieces.

When I delve into my friends and family's closets I love revealing what they are missing. It's always a lightbulb moment. As well as discovering fresh new combinations of clothes you already own, it's important to work out what the gaps are, and often what the cause of those gaps is. When you realize what you need it can open up a whole load of new opportunities for outfits. The gaps in your wardrobe will make it hard to create new combinations, and if you have any pieces that you haven't worn much (and who doesn't?) it's likely that they remain unworn because you're missing something to go with them. I bet your unworn items will be statement makers, something you fell in love with for their boldness. The pieces I rarely wear are all evening-y, glamorous and in colours far beyond my usual palette of navy and charcoal. Perhaps you have a pair of teal leather culottes or a brocade tunic dress that lies untouched? No-one leaves a navy crew-neck sweater unworn for months, do they?

Work out what your dream outfit is with that statement piece, then make a shopping list of what will help you fulfil the goal. And then shop for it. Ensure that the new piece will go with at least another two pieces that you already own, because you don't want to end up with *another* wardrobe white elephant. And then make an outfit! Check also that you have enough basic building blocks. These aren't the most exciting items to shop for, but ensuring that you have black and skin-tone camisoles and bras to wear with sheer tops, white shirts, T-shirts and simple tailored trousers in dark and neutral tones, will go a long way to making dressing a pain-free experience.

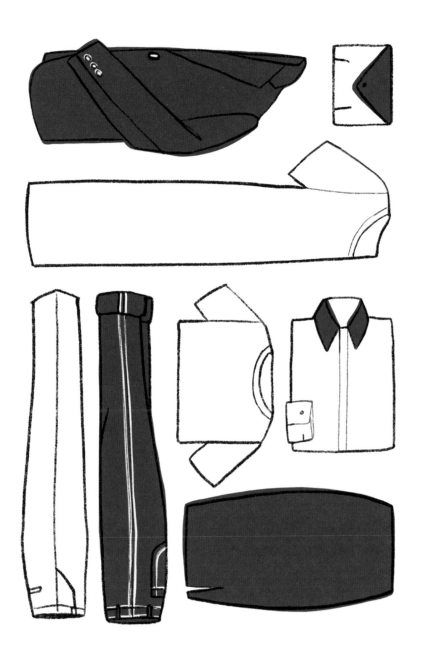

CAPSULE WARDROBES

There are some schools of thought that say you only need a few pieces to create a functional working wardrobe. We've spoken about the key items you should own (see pages 44–55) but I would never suggest that they are *all* you should rely on. They all work together, but if that was all you could wear, life would be very boring indeed. This book is certainly not about fashion abstinence. All kinds of numbers – 7, 28, 37, even 48 – have been lauded as the magic number of pieces that will make up the ultimate capsule wardrobe, but personally I couldn't live with such austerity and such restrictions. I also couldn't deny myself the pleasure of shopping; I'm a sybarite and have very little willpower. The intention is a good one: if you know what you own, and wear it, it will be easier to get dressed in the morning. There are also far too many purchases going to waste in the Western world. To keep on top of being tidy in a small space, the 'one in, one out' policy will come in handy, and the principles of building a capsule wardrobe in which everything goes with everything else *is* appealing. However, I recommend allowing yourself the pleasure of new-season updates and playing with trends every once in a while, too.

THE CLEAR-OUT

At some point, however cleverly and calmly you shop, it will be time for a wardrobe detox. Some methods of editing are brutal. If you don't wear it, it instantly goes the way of the charity shop. This brings me out in a cold sweat. If you've invested in items that still fit you and look good, and you have a varied enough lifestyle to ensure they will get worn, I believe there can still be a place for them in your wardrobe, even if you only wear them once or twice a year. It's like the seasonal switchover: you don't have to wear something to the point of wearing it out in order to justify keeping it. If it's not in a seasonal box, archive it. Special pieces that have memories attached to them should be kept if you are of a sentimental nature. I am. And pieces that will only work for certain occasions (a black tie ball, for example) don't have to be binned, if you have space for them. If you can store your irregularly worn clothes in suitcases layered with tissue paper and lavender bags, I recommend it. However, if you're a little more pragmatic and are keen to embrace a more minimalistic wardrobe, these are the questions to ask of each item.

1 Does it fit me?
There is absolutely no point in keeping an item that you will never again squeeze into, or which hangs off you like a bin bag. If it is of huge sentimental value (the dress you wore when you met your partner, perhaps) it can be archived.

2 Did I wear it this season?
If you skipped wearing that sundress this summer or didn't pull out that cosy knit last winter, you're unlikely to wear it next year. Put it away for six months, and if you don't get excited about seeing it next time round, it should go.

3 Is it clean? Is it in good condition?
If you can get something dry-cleaned and repaired within a week, it can stay (if you want to wear it, that is). If taking it to the dry-cleaners ends up as a glaringly overlooked item on your to-do list and the piece waits in purgatory for a month, it's likely you won't wear

it even when it *is* spruced up and ready to wear. If it's a super-special party dress, you could clean it and archive it, if you absolutely must. But note the difference between clothes that need to be repaired (for example, if there is a button missing) but are still in good condition, and those that are tired and worn out. Anything overly bobbled or that has shiny cuffs or foxing on the collar where it's starting to fray, will never make you look good when you wear it, however much you might love it. Exhausted items should be retired from your wardrobe.

4 Do I feel like me in it? Do I forget I'm wearing it?
The best pieces in your wardrobe should allow you to go and live your life without having to stop and hitch up the straps, smooth down your skirt or hoik up the neckline. You have to feel confident and comfortable in your outfits at all times, however fabulous a piece might be.

5 Does it spark joy?

To borrow Marie Kondo's famous mantra, does the thought of wearing it make you happy? Are you excited about going out in that item or are you worried about what knickers to wear underneath it or the agony those heels might cause? Even if it's a basic T-shirt, you should feel happy to touch it and pleased you have found the best essential building block for your wardrobe.

6 Can I make up three outfits with it from items I already own?

If you can't, that's OK, because doing a wardrobe clear-out will definitely reveal some gaping holes. However, if in a month's time those gaps remained unfilled and you *still* can't create any outfits to show off that lonesome skirt to its best advantage, perhaps it should go to a new home.

If you're still undecided about what should stay and what should go, the next step is the holding-pen system. I pull out any of the pieces I am on the fence about keeping. If it's hanging on the outside of my wardrobe and fully visible, then I will be inclined to build an outfit from it. When I do wear it, if I can't wait to get home and tear it off at the end of the day, it has to go. Or else it slips back into the wardrobe to be worn another day.

One other clever method I use as a halfway house between the reality of keeping things or chucking them is the hanger switch. If there are clothes you're attached to, and that have survived the interrogation above, but you *still* haven't worn them, put the hanger on the rail facing the wrong way. If the hanger still remains back to front in a year's time, it's time to visit the charity shop, eBay or a designer resale site, such as VestiaireCollective. com. Some experts may advise a six-month timeframe but I don't want to hassle you into a decision you will regret, and besides, you need to have the opportunity of a whole year's weather before you decide what to do with that piece. During this time, hopefully you can make a purchase that will enable you to wear the piece and get the hanger facing the right way again.

As you go through the year, try to have a mini editing session of your wardrobe every month. You will be able to do imperceptible switches for warmer and cooler clothing as the seasons shift and can keep on top of any gaps that may arise. You will also be able to mix in any new buys with ease. Maybe that's just one piece a month, but it will keep everything looking fresh and mean you won't need to go crazy in the shops for a full new-season splurge twice a year.

A WORD ON MOTHS

I almost cannot bring myself to type the word since the great mothpocalypse of 2008. As well as being the year I was was made redundant and the financial markets crashed worldwide, I remember it painfully for being the year clothes moths attacked my wardrobe.

It was my own fault. I bought a pair of vintage sheepskin-lined ice-skating boots at a car boot sale and took them into my house to use as a styling prop. I did give them a clean before I took them home, but as I wasn't planning on actually wearing them (they were purely to hang on a faux-antler coat hook in the hall) I didn't think they would need to be disinfected. How wrong I was. I started to notice a few fluttery culprits, and then a couple of holes. I am a make-do-and-mender so I did some handy sewing work, but when more and more clothes were affected, I couldn't ignore it. I didn't want to believe that I was a victim of moths: I know this sounds melodramatic, but it felt like more than an attack on my wardrobe. As clothes are so intertwined with my life and loves, it was a personal attack too! I went bananas and bought mothballs, cedar balls and lavender, but it wasn't enough. I'd read that moths are put off by strong smells, but my infestation was so tenacious they actually ate through a cashmere lavender pouch. The only thing that helped was getting Rentokil in for three weeks of intense treatments in my home, dry-cleaning my clothes and leaving others in the freezer for a fortnight. I was a broken woman. I still remember some of the clothing casualties with a pang of regret for all the good times we could have had together, but I resolved to be strong and keep shopping – just not for vintage ice-skating boots. Now any second-hand textiles will go straight into the freezer (double wrapped in plastic bags) as the cold will kill any eggs or larvae. Dry-cleaning will also have the same effect, but depending on how much vintage you like to buy, it can get expensive.

Incidentally, I've also learned that putting fluffy mohair sweaters in the freezer overnight before you plan on wearing them will help prevent the wool from shedding. It won't last all day, and by lunchtime you may need a lint roller handy, but it's a helpful tip. Likewise, there are some denim aficionados who never wash their jeans and simply put them in the freezer to freshen them up. The cold will kill any bacteria and smells, and not putting them through the washing machine or chemical-laden dry-clean cycle will ensure that the dark indigo wash remains as intense and blue as the day you bought them.

SECRET

STYLING

TRICKS

SECRET STYLING TRICKS

The reason that fashion folk always look put together, even if they are aiming for an artfully dishevelled look, is the styling. On shoots and at the shows, in designers' studios – when you're surrounded by people whose career is based on making clothes look good (and are obsessed with fashion, too) it's impossible not to pick up some tips on how to elevate an outfit from basic to styled. Away from the catwalk, you don't want to look like a fashion victim (because it *is* possible to be over-styled): the goal is to take an average outfit and pimp it a little bit. As a teenager, before I landed my dream job on a magazine, I would spend hours just trying on my wardrobe (and some choice pieces from my mother's closet, too.) Practice makes perfect, and this valuable time spent working out what went together and what didn't, and how my clothes could say more about me in a second than I ever could in person, meant it was not a wasted youth. It also kept me away from the back of the bike sheds. Now, in my day job as a stylist, I can pick out the plainest pieces and give them a little twist that makes the outfit work brilliantly and feel much more put together, whether it's on a model or a 'real' person.

THE HIGH-LOW MIX

If there's one trick that will take you from simply wearing clothes to looking styled, it's adopting the secret formula of fashion insiders for choosing outfits that look perfectly put together.

Imagine you've turned up to a party and totally swerved the dress code. A nightmare scenario, but would you rather be the one in a ball gown in a sea of blue jeans, or the denim clad rebel in a room full of cocktail dresses? I'd definitely prefer to be in jeans. Looking overdressed is one of the stylish set's biggest fears and trying too hard is fashion anathema. It's for good reason. A head-to-toe look or matching handbag and shoes is just not cool.

But this doesn't mean dressing down or adopting a scruffy demeanour to ensure you never look flashy. Instead, dress high *and* low, an ingenious method that everyone in

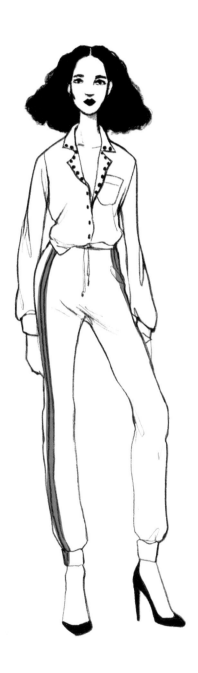

the industry swears by to balance out the most fabulous pieces in your wardrobe with the most mundane. You will always fit in with every occasion and this clever equation allows you to get extra wear from those things you bought for special occasions only.

In essence, high–low dressing boils down to a simple formula: Take one part crazy (a brocade cocktail skirt) and one part plain (a block-colour T-shirt) and team them together to give your outfit an unexpected twist. The surprise element of fancy mixed with your basic wardrobe staples will look considered but never calculated, and you win major points for creative styling. It's why silky blouses look freshest with beaten-up denim jeans rather than equally silky skirts, and the reason a leather jacket looks eternally cool over a sequinned slip dress and canvas sneakers.

As long as you keep a ratio of 50:50, sticking to the perfect balance of high and low, your outfits will always work. It's foolproof. And keep the formula in mind when you're choosing accessories, too. The wrong shoe can throw your outfit totally out of kilter. You can balance out a whole look – say, a T-shirt and jeans (low) with an evening clutch and strappy heels (high) – or choose fancy silk trousers and a similarly posh handbag (both high) worn with sneakers and a plain button-down shirt (both low). The creativity is in the mix.

If you're looking to nail the look in one item, a shortcut to easy high–low style is to pick a very fancy shoe style but choose a flat, such as Gucci's iconic Princetown loafers in rich brocade. The fabric looks like something straight out of the court of Versailles, but because they are in a classic flat loafer silhouette they easily pass for dressed-down daywear.

Print and plain fabrics are also something you should should mix in a 50:50 high–low ratio. The ideal outfit would mix something patterned with a block colour-piece, but if you're feeling bold, two prints can go together if they have a similar base shade (perhaps they're both on a black background) and the patterns are of contrasting sizes. So a tiny sprig-print blouse with an oversized design skirt would work. Giant, genetically modified florals on trousers *and* top would veer into dangerous territory. Be aware that your accessories in any printed outfit will have to be very dialled-down to counterbalance the pattern play and keep your outfit on the cool side of clashing.

I wore a denim Current Elliott shirt with a leopard-print Topshop skirt to Milan Fashion Week and had a street-style photographer chase me three blocks to get a picture of the outfit. I had teamed it with a Gucci tank top to elevate the look even more, which brings me to the next essential styling tip...

My other favourite combinations include:
Denim jacket + lace slip dress
Grey sweatshirt + silk trousers
Jewel-trimmed blouse + tracksuit bottoms
Tuxedo jacket + jeans
Chambray shirt + leopard-print skirt

THE THIRD PIECE

This mythical method, which elevates one piece to saviour status, originated in the US, where sales assistants are often advised to wear three pieces as part of their uniform, and to also add one thing to shoppers' outfits in the fitting room to transform the look of an outfit from simple to styled.

The concept is pretty basic. Even if you're not a fan of maths, it's worth learning off by heart and will serve you far better than trigonometry. Take a top and a bottom, whether it's a skirt, jeans or trousers, and add one other item to transform the outfit's mood. It's *soooo* easy. You'll look more polished, edgier or glamorous depending on what outerwear or accessory you choose. Note that shoes and bags don't count towards your three-piece total, but they can make a vital difference to the overall look. Technically, belts can be the third piece but I advise always wearing a belt, so for me it doesn't count.

Let's take some examples of how the third piece can change your look.

Start with a white shirt and dark leather skirt. What are you going to wear with them? Slip a faded music T-shirt under the shirt (and leave the shirt mainly unbuttoned) or pull on a fuschia satin blazer: each addition will take the outfit to a totally different place, but both will elevate it from the basic. A slouchy khaki cardigan or glittering crystal chandelier earrings will have the same effect with very different results.

What about a white T-shirt and mid-blue washed jeans: a classic combination? Yes, but one that can certainly be improved upon. A sharply tailored double-breasted jacket adds business flair, while a plaid shirt makes it look grunge, especially if you tie it around the waist. A heavily beaded statement necklace or ribbon choker dresses the outfit up in a different direction, too.

A trouser-suit combo of jacket and trousers could be your first two items, but the third piece – what lies beneath – is crucial. A sheer blouse takes it to cocktails, a crisp button-down shirt works for the boardroom, a slouchy linen T-shirt would look edgy when worn with sneakers. Or, depending on the cut of the jacket, you could go daringly bare and just tie a long, skinny silk scarf around your neck, *à la* Mick Jagger in his prime.

THE GOLDEN RULE

If you take just one piece of advice from this book, there is a rule you should always stick to when getting dressed. Never, ever, *ever*, wear one brand head-to-toe. If you can, try to make sure every item in an outfit is from a different place. In the magazine industry there are many cruel insults used to describe someone dressed entirely in one catwalk look. The harshest disses mean that no imagination or consideration went into the chosen outfit. It's as box fresh as the designer intended: dull and safe. Better to be the old woman that wears purple and a red hat ('that doesn't suit her') than to have perpetually good taste. As the late photographer Helmut Newton opined, 'it's the worst thing that can happen to a creative person'.

When you're getting dressed in the morning it's easy to reach for your current favourites, but as you build the day's outfit always remember where each piece is from. On more occasions than I care to remember I've nearly ended up leaving the house in a Zara dress, shoes and jacket... disaster! Even if they're from different seasons and different stores it implies a laziness while getting dressed that doesn't sit happily with the well-styled.

I remember shopping with my mother as a child (there were many outings to the shops) and the sales assistants would always put outfits together to entice her to buy the whole look. The idea of dressing yourself well is to develop a personal style that cannot be bought off the rack and worn head to toe. Perhaps you really do love the blouse, skirt and jacket that hang next to each other in store in equal measure, but promise me that you'll never wear them together. I also see this rule as a little rebellion against the tricks of the store merchandizers. They will put clothes that go together, such as complementary tops and bottoms, next to each other to try to increase sales. Being aware of this cunning way of making money makes me rail against their methods even more. I'm keen to create my own personal style every time I get dressed.

THE FINAL TRICKS OF THE TRADE

Once you've got your clothes on and your outfit ready to go, there are a few further elements to consider. These tricks will add extra panache to your look.

TUCK / UNTUCK

When I was at school, tucking your shirt in was for geeks, but leaving it out would risk detention. Being good girls and boys, we developed an ingenious way of rolling the hem so it was just caught by our waistbands and billowed out almost as though it was untucked. There was also a weird craze for doing up only the bottom button on your cardigan, but the less said about that the better.

However, there are plenty of less sloppy ways to make your shirts look less formal but still feel pulled together. It's called the 'tuck/untuck'. There are two ways to do it. The first works with shirts and involves tucking in the fabric on one half of the placket (where the buttons are stitched) from the middle of your waist to a couple of inches away from your hip, while the other half blows free all the way round to your opposite hip.

One step smarter is this. Once your bottoms are done up and your top is on, place your hands halfway between belly button and hip on each side of your waist. Slide the fabric under your hands – and the material between the hands – under the waistband so you're tucked in. The shirting from the hips outwards remains free for that perfectly imperfect look, while your waist is defined and you look casually polished. You'll see every one of the street-style stars working a tuck/untuck at fashion week. I just wish we'd worked out how to get away with it at school.

ARM ROLL

Ah, the artful rolled sleeve, bringing insouciant glamour to silk shirts everywhere. But there is a method to the madness of shortening a full-length sleeve for fashion's sake. Don't just roll your sleeve up to elbow height or you'll look like a Young Farmer gone wrong. That's far too basic. There is a special fashion insider's way to perfect the sleeve and it goes like this: Take the hem of your shirt sleeve and fold it up, bringing it all the way up to your bicep. Next, take the bottom folded edge of your sleeve and fold it up once or twice until it hits just above your elbow. Pull out the cuff at the outer edge – the arm equivalent of popping your collar – and you're done: immaculately rolled sleeves.

BELT IT!

I'm an advocate for belting every single outfit you wear. With any pair of jeans or trousers, or in fact anything with belt loops, the addition of a belt will ensure that your outfit has a basic level of styling. You could (and probably will) be in jeans, T-shirt and flip-flops at some point, but wearing a belt will make it feel less flung on, even if you picked your clothes up off the floor. (And that's not a fashion don't, by the way.) Belts do far more than hold your trousers up. They offer a glimpse of your style personality, whether you choose black patent or beaten-up tan leather, and can create a nipped-in waist on even the most un-defined figures. At the moment fashion is having a love affair with the waist. Through the seasons and the years, different body parts are the focus of our attention, whether cleavage, legs, ribs (really) through sweetheart necklines and cut-out details, or mini-skirt lengths. While its placement will rise and fall from hips to belly button, and its width will range from wide to narrow, a belt is always in fashion.

Your trench coat will come with a soft fabric belt, but however much you want to protect yourself from the elements, never buckle it up; instead, tie it in a 'stylist's knot'. It's not the sort of skill you'll learn in the Brownies, but its far more useful. Here's the how-to: Tie your belt in a simple knot, slightly off to one side of your waist. Loop one end as if you are going to make a bow, then wrap the other end around the base to secure it. Pull it tight. Fan out the loop at the top, then arrange the two loose ends pointing downwards at a jaunty angle. I've seen advice that suggests swapping out the belt the trench comes with for one of your own, but please don't do that. It looks try-hard and agonizingly considered, which is the complete opposite of what a throw-it-on, effortlessly elegant trench should be. Sometimes a dress, shorts, skirt or even a shirt will come ready-to-wear with belt attached, and for these items you can feel free to play with the styling. I would always advise swapping to one of your own belts – adding a punkish twist to a prim shift dress or making city shorts perfect weekend wear. Just leave the trench belt alone.

If you thought a belt could only be fastened by its buckle, think again: there's one more way to style this accessory. This works on softer materials and pliable leather. Start by threading the end through the buckle as normal, then instead of tucking it through the belt loop as usual, take it below the belt and loop it under itself. Bring it back to the front and pop the tail through the loop you've created to make a knot. Again, this little trick will make your simplest outfits look a little more raw in style. I most recently did it on a shoot over a leopard-print coat to give the fancy uptown polish a downtown edge, but it works brilliantly on the street too.

HOW TO LAYER

During the seventeen years I have worked on magazines, every autumn, without fail, my colleagues and editors would beg me to create a feature on how to layer. In a world affected by climate change, and one ruled by fierce central heating, equally boisterous air conditioning units and unhealthily hot public transport, layering is the solution. But the problem with layering is that it has, by its very nature, the potential to add bulk to any body shape. So the solution is to choose many fine, light layers, and to pick your top and bottom layers with care.

Starting from the bottom, Uniqlo's Heattech range has been a lifesaver on many a chilly outdoor location shoot, and in some freezing empty warehouses in east London too! The fabric has a clever way of trapping body heat and storing it close to your skin to keep you warm. A T-shirt and leggings are the ultimate layers to slip into (over your underwear) when the weather is really icy. Alternatively, silk is renowned for its insulating properties. Just make sure that whatever layers you start with are fitted close to your body to keep a slim silhouette as you add more clothes. Be aware that if you're going to mainly be inside, these layers will be too warm, so concentrate on adding extra warmth from your final, easily removed layer instead.

The ultimate layering item has to be the polo neck. In cotton jersey they add a sleek element to even the most practical outfit, especially in beatnik, Audrey Hepburn-esque black. However, I like a charcoal grey or navy version too, or a subtle fine stripe, which make the top look like it's a styled element of my outfit, rather than just a layer to keep me warm. Polo necks look fantastic under shirts left unbuttoned to below the bust line, or floaty, flirty dresses. They look streetwise and tough under a sporty sweatshirt yet slightly plain if you wear them beneath a crew-neck knit, so choose a top or dress that has a placket to add interest to the top half of your outfit. Again, it's really important to choose a sleek polo neck rather than a chunky knitted version because it will make the upper layers sit far more smoothly.

The next layer will be the statement-maker of your outfit. Whether you pick a bold full skirt, a flannel shirt, a sharp shift dress or a printed jumpsuit, these are the pieces that people will focus on. When you are planning what to wear, this is the layer you should start with. Your layers below and on top should complement this core outfit, so choose colours, print and texture that enhance the design details and style of your look. You can also pick clever, season-less clothes. By putting extra clothes below and above this layer, you can get far more mileage out of a skimpy summer sundress or lightweight cotton pieces, and wear things that give you happy summer memories during the darkest months. Even though the idea of layering is to choose several pieces that you can add to, this layer, and the ones that sit below below, are pretty certain to remain in place during the day.

Depending on how much cold you need to protect yourself from, you can add a cardigan. Whether that's a super-sized fluffy mohair monster that comes down to your knees or a polite and lightweight merino wool V-neck version, depends on the rest of your outfit as well as the weather. A thick, chunky knit will be the item that adds the most bulk to a layered look, so keeping your outfit in proportion is paramount. A clean silhouette, such as cigarette pants and mini skirts, will be the natural partner to chunky cardis that end at mid-thigh, and won't put your look out of kilter in the way that a wide-leg trouser or mid-length skirt would. Conversely, a leaner knit can take a bolder shape on your bottom half, and Oxford bags or pleated skirts will look best. Cardigans slip in and out of fashion; they enjoyed huge popularity in the late 1990s, thanks to the designer boutique Voyage, who created cardigans that were encrusted with a mad haberdashers' psychedelic dreamscape. They are currently back in vogue, but whatever the trends dictate, ensure that you add a cardigan that works with your personal style.

When you're building up layers, it's easy to concentrate on the top half of an outfit, but what lies below the waist can be layered just as cleverly. Jeans are a great starting point, and when worn under a swirling chiffon skirt they have a great play of movement. The skirt or dress should be split to the thigh to allow for maximum movement, and the most current style of jeans is faded mid-blue and straight leg. Over-the-knee boots have a sexy reputation, but a flat pair can add vital warmth to an outfit if you feel the need to wear a skirt. Nothing clothes-wise will keep your knees as cosy as a pair of boots.

A common complaint when you're layered up to this level is that you feel that you're drowning in fabric. How to accessorize an outfit like that? The good old belt. Cinch it in at the waist, over the cardigan, to remind the world – and yourself – that you have a waist. By pulling in the excess fabric you will feel more polished and look sharper – although, if your lower layers sit close to your body, as advised, it shouldn't really be necessary.

A word on gilets, *aka* sleeveless jackets or waistcoats. Although they're much derided for being worn by a certain type of school-run mum, I'm actually a fan of the gilet. The navy quilted version certainly looks like you're all set for Pony Club camp, and the shaggy griege sheepskin version (worn with tight white jeans and a very expensive, very glossy head of blonde highlights) are both clichés in the extreme. But how about a black sheepskin gilet, or a longline sleeveless denim jacket, or even a knitted jerkin? The anti-gilet brigade complain that they are pointless, as they have nothing to keep your arms warm, but I find they allow you to complete the supermarket shop, a busy work day or a bracing weekend walk without feeling weighed down by a cumbersome jacket. Especially when teamed with a cardigan: you can be just as warm as you would be in a jacket, but you will look just that bit more styled. Keep in mind that you will need to add edge, perhaps with a pair of studded boots, some ripped denim or a slogan sweatshirt, to tone down the mumsiness of the gilet. A favourite way to wear a gilet is over a leather biker jacket. When you get to your destination, take both jacket and gilet off. I once wore this combination to a wedding where the dress code was rock 'n' roll, and felt at once louche and warm while we posed for pictures in the street.

For the final layer, the icing on the cake, finish with a coat. During winter it's likely your friends will see your coat more than they see your normal clothes, so always make sure that your top layer fits your style MO. If you're looking for a coat that will really keep you warm, leather or pleather are sure-fire winners, and always look for a coat with a lining. The cleverest coats are puffer jackets, which are down-filled and super warm. They will keep you cosy on the street, but will squash up small for the commute. Because they are usually covered with a synthetic coating, puffers have a brilliant tendency not to wrinkle, which means you won't look as though you just pulled your crushed-up coat out of a carrier bag, even if you did. Max Mara's down-filled Cube coats even fit into their own small pouches, so maximum space is saved.

Layering should be easy to get right if you follow these guidelines. Bear in mind the main lesson of keeping your outfit in proportion, and choose pieces that sit as close to your body, and each other, as possible, to build a streamlined silhouette. As the day warms up, the outer layers of coats and cardigans can be removed, and if you really find yourself sweltering, your outfit will still work as a whole if you slip out of your polo neck.

HOW TO NAVIGATE THE TRENDS AND STEER CLEAR OF SILLY ONES

Every season it's my job to plan which clothes (and shoes, bags and accessories) that have appeared on the catwalk will constitute a trend. And then from those trends, I filter out what is pure catwalk fantasy, what is a trickle-down phenomenon (one which will eventually make it to the street once the high street's eyes have adjusted) and what will blow up as a wear-it-now mega-trend.

What you see in the media (and this includes traditional and social media) will have undergone the same editing process. Each title or channel will have their own criteria and will present what is appropriate for their viewers or readership, so what you might see in, say, *i-D* magazine will be very different from the way *Harper's Bazaar* translates the trends. In the same way that each title filters what does and doesn't work for them and their reader's lifestyles, you should learn to only take on the trends that will fit your life and your existing wardrobe.

I get to see trends emerge first-hand at the international catwalk shows in New York, London, Milan and Paris, but vogue.com, the Vogue Runway app and countless editors and bloggers will publish pictures of a designer's collection on Instagram as it happens – so you can get a glimpse of trends as they break, too. At each show or presentation I will take notes (and snap photos or make sketches as an *aide-memoir*) and study the new collection, marking down fabrics, silhouettes, lengths and details. My notes will be as basic as 'red', 'shirts with extra', or 'very Mod', and then I might add in one or two bad sketches to reiterate the shape or detail those 'very Mod' details. As I go round the designers' showrooms or sit through more shows, I might notice that I'm using those same words again, or a completely different set.

You could do something similar by going round a department store, picking one department and focusing on colour trends or fabrics to begin with, and noticing the retail trends in that area. Your eyes and mind will start to pick up on the prevalent shades and shapes, and as they become more apparent you will be able to crown them as bona fide trends. It's fun to wander down Oxford Street, noticing how many cropped T-shirts or pink coats you see, and tallying up whether they count as a trend. There's an old cliché that says 'one is an example, two is a coincidence and three makes a trend', although I like to make sure that at least five brands are doing something to ensure it counts.

Trends are cyclical, so as sure as hemlines will rise, they will drop. Brands will likely follow a dark season, colour-wise, with a light one. Trend prediction companies look at overall lifestyle moods and their impact on fashion to work out what we will probably be wearing two or three years from now. It's not a mystical art, but a rather pragmatic one, and you can trace a clear arc when you sit down and follow the clues. I find that individual designers follow a trajectory that either sees their style evolving slowly, season by season, creeping with imperceptible change, or it ricocheting in the opposite direction each time. Christopher Kane, the Scottish-born, London-based designer, is the latter kind of talent. You can never be sure which way his new season will go, whether he will choose embellishment, focus on fabrics, choose crazy colour or add wild print, whereas other designers' work can be far easier to predict.

There will always be a high-end or from-the-street trend that subtly makes itself known but is too weird for real life. Keep an eye on it, or wear it first, if that's what you like to do. What seems fashion-forward or 'out there' now will slowly make its way into the mainstream. If you start to focus your eyes and adopt some of the tools the professionals have access to, you'll start your trend-prediction journey. But, crucially, you still need to know what to avoid if you want to shop the trends. If you've identified your personal style, it should be easy to work out which trends will fit into your wardrobe. If you see one item everywhere on the catwalk or all over the shops, you can guarantee it will be a one-season wonder and quickly turn old. You might have had a fling with an off-the-shoulder Bardot top last summer, but now it will feel dated. Sticking to your own style will be far more fulfilling, even though there's nothing more annoying than your signature style becoming an 'It' item. Revel in the knowledge that imitation is surely the sincerest form of fashion flattery.

FASHION
IS
FUN

FASHION IS FUN

To conclude this book, I want to make sure you know that feeling great in your clothes is of the upmost importance. Sharing the tips and tricks from my professional life in the previous chapters should help make getting dressed easier, faster and less expensive, whether you came here to learn how to roll the perfect sleeve or stop buying things you'll never take out of the wardrobe. If you forget what you're wearing, it's a good clothes day. I'll leave it to you whether that's a pink tutu or pinstriped trouser suit – and if it's the former, thank you for making me smile on the bus!

Fashion gets a bad rap. It's an industry, and a serious business; sometimes it's hard to remember to smile when you're trying to sell clothes. Fashion is neither a frivolous distraction from the political traumas of our time, nor is it flippantly blasé about society's bigger issues. It's both a reflection of and escape from the world we are surrounded by. And it *is* fun. If you can make a difference to the mood of your day through what you wear, and even better to that of others around you, fashion will have done its job.

If you can dress up when you want to (supermarket shop included) and resolve never to save your best for best, you're going to make it in style. Although there are times when even your best might not be dressy enough. Enter the dreaded dress code...

DECODING THE DRESS CODE

There have been many times, when an invitation has pinged into my inbox, that I have felt despair spread into the pit of my stomach because of the ridiculous dress code attached. I've been lucky enough to attend an array of events and know the inside track on what the expectations attached to each dress code are, but my personal opinion is that dress codes should be done away with. They are old-fashioned and out-dated. They stifle personal style and, even if you do helpfully include some direction on your invitation, some guests will ignore it anyway. Better to offer a simple direction such as 'Dress up' or 'We're keeping it laid back' than a confusing amalgamation of codes. I once worked with an ex-editor of a society magazine who was appalled by the 'dress up' instruction, but if you're not going to get hung up on dress lengths and traditional rules for wearing gloves, I think it offers the clearest direction that the party giver is going to put on a show, and hopes you will too. On the other hand, 'Dressy-casual-cocktail' is *not* going to help your indecisive attendees know what to wear. More effective dress codes offer hints to the venue and style of the event as well.

Wherever you're headed, you should look at the invitation itself, and the venue, for clues. Have you been invited to a stately home via a stiff chunk of gilt-edged card embossed with a swirly copperplate font, or sent an email invitation to meet at the local brasserie, or did you simply get a text the week before? That implies a high level of casualness and that the hosts won't mind what you arrive in. Helpful hosts include an idea of dress on the invitation to allow guests plenty of time to plan an outfit and also to anticipate the occasion's sartorial mood. I've outlined the traditional, expected and obvious choices for each below, along with an idea for a wild-card outfit that will still tick any specific rules that need to be adhered to, while allowing you to stand out in a sea of raven-like LBDs.

One thing you should always consider is whether to plan your outfit with your date or the friends you will be going with. If you look similarly styled, in tonal colours or a matching array of silhouettes, then you will feel much more appropriate.

As well as traditional dress codes that apply to one event only, beware the member's club and their year-round draconian door policies. I particularly despise the banned item, something clubs are famed for. No jeans, no trainers, no sportswear – whole brands dismissed! OK, sometimes football hooligans may gravitate towards a certain label as a uniform but on one memorable occasion, at a tea party hosted at member's club in Mayfair, there was a directive of 'no leather or suede'. Shoes and bags were allowed, but a chic leather pencil skirt (like the below-knee Tom Ford for YSL one I found on eBay and treasure) or tailored suede blazer (I'm thinking of the beautiful chestnut-brown one that my chic mother wears on smart days out) were outlawed. I do understand that both the venue and the hosts wanted to preserve a certain level of elegance, and that sweat-stained leggings and muscle vests worn straight from the gym were a no-no, but to actively cull a style or lob a particular fabric into the banned box feels dated and draconian. If your jeans were Gucci's dreamy appliquéd numbers you would be showing a lot more respect than you would if you turned up in a Bri-nylon shirt, just because it had a collar.

WHAT DO DRESS CODES MEAN?

When faced with an invitation with a dress code attached, here is the definitive guide to what to wear when.

WHITE TIE

It's the rarest of dress codes and the most formal. It's likely you'll only come across white tie on film (period-drama directors love a white-tie ball scene) but in the real world, if you're invited to a state ball, royal event, charity do, very posh wedding or party thrown by Elton John, it will be white tie. It's also known as 'full evening dress' or simply 'tails' if you're being casual about it – but make no mistake, white tie is anything but casual! When planning your outfit you can go as glitzy, glamorous, bejewelled or decadent as you like. It's got to be long, but you could go strapless. Print is discouraged, so choose a plain block colour (an ice blue would offset the white jackets the men must wear) and always wear jewels. Tiaras should only be worn if you're married, though. You should also wear gloves at all times, apart from when you're eating (even if it's just a canapé), and don't leave unworn gloves on the table; tuck them under your napkin on your lap. If you don't want to wear long gloves, leave them off entirely rather than go for a short pair. The ridiculous original direction was for women to show their décolletage, but I would ignore this because it's perverse and misogynistic, unless of course you want to. If you've been invited to such a fancy do, the hosts are likely to really stand on ceremony and will notice if you go off-piste in your choices, so this is the one time you shouldn't be tempted to push the boundaries and wear a short cocktail frock or floaty maxi dress. One last note: when you're wearing something so fancy, a day coat will ruin the look, so find an evening coat or cape to accompany the glamour.

BLACK TIE

If your event starts after 7 p.m., this is the most likely dress-code directive you'll receive, and it's common for city weddings and night-time receptions, especially at stately homes or hotels. The female guidelines for black tie were invented simply to complement the male guests at balls and galas, who would be in black dinner jackets, so that is why black dresses are the most usual choice. Technically you should go long, but if you think cleverly you can subvert the norm. It doesn't *have* to be a dress, and a floor-length ball skirt would look particularly modern, especially when worn with a crisp cotton shirt, like the glamourous Venezuelan designer Carolina Herrera does. Or you could choose something short. If you prefer your legs to your arms, then certainly avoid a long dress but perhaps pick one with a high neckline, dramatic backless detail or sweeping statement sleeves. As long as you add statement accessories, such as a jewelled necklace to fill in the collar-line, small silk clutch and glamorous shoes, it will tick the black tie box. Think about what you'd wear to the Oscars and aim for elevated evening glamour.

Always adapt the dress code to your own personal style. If you're sporty, then simple lines and streamlined silhouettes will work for you and the fabrics you choose will give an after-dark edge. Likewise, if you like bohemian daywear, choose a silhouette that feels 'you' – perhaps a skirt full of tiers of silk or a full peasant sleeve – and add accessories that nod to your own tastes.

If you want to push the dress code further, you could wear a fitted black velvet tuxedo suit with a sheer black blouse and heels. Steer clear of print, which looks lairy and day-time in such a formal setting. Bold block tones in silk or taffeta are best and you can choose any shade you want – a pop of primary colour will add drama to proceedings. Tights are a traditional requirement but they make the coolest outfit look frumpy as well as making even the slinkiest of dresses ride up, so either go for an on-trend super-sheer black 10 denier pair (if your dress is short) or be modern in bare legs. Just remember, when you're shopping for a black-tie dress, it's not something you'd wear on any old Saturday night out. Think fancy, formal and red carpet-worthy.

MORNING DRESS

This is the default dress code for weddings in churches and any event during the so called 'season' that starts before 6 p.m. It's sometimes called 'formal day dress' and you should keep modesty at the forefront of your mind. Black-tie events are likely to be more debauched in attitude (to put it bluntly, it's evening, so there will be alcohol involved) so you can get away with challenging the rules, but at a morning-dress do there's nowhere to hide. Long sleeves and midi lengths are preferable; wear with heels in the city or a garden-party-appropriate flat for the country. Knees should be covered, whether it's a skirt, dress or jumpsuit, and your top half should have thick straps or sleeves, nothing strapless or spaghetti-strapped. Jumpsuits are a brilliantly bold choice and currently one of the most fashionable, too.

Although you don't have to wear a jacket, at any summer event in the UK you will probably need one for warmth. A slouchy double-breasted blazer in a pale shade will be best. Cardigans are currently back in favour, so you could wear one instead of a scarf, but the pashmina is useful only as a blankie on transatlantic flights (cut the tassels off, like Sienna Miller did). A hat is something of a necessity for morning dress but check the venue's individual dress code.

If you're heading to the races at Ascot, get out your ruler to measure the base and ensure that it counts as a hat, not a fascinator. Try on lots of styles in a department store to find out what suits you, but a straw boater (such as one from French milliner Maison Michel) would be the cool choice, if it works on your face. Fascinators are far too prissy and, although she's often cited as style maven, the Duchess of Cambridge should not be your inspiration for morning dress if you want to have any semblance of fashionability in your outfit. The men will likely be wearing grey tones as part of their suits, so pastels immediately make sense as a colour choice, as do soft florals. Anything with a tropical print will feel vulgar.

GARDEN PARTY

In the US, this dress code takes its style notes from morning dress, without the formalities of British tradition, so you can do away with hats and straps on your dress. Choose cocktail or tea-length dresses and think flowy shapes, simple silhouettes and lightweight fabrics in pale colours or soft florals.

LOUNGE SUITS

Despite the tantalizing direction to lounge, this will still be a smart and formal event, such as a city dinner party, business do or wedding. Men will be in business suits and ties and women are expected to be similarly polished. That could mean a sharply cut cocktail dress, elegantly mismatched separates or a suit, but smart and chic are the watchwords. For these events, the 18-hour dress will be your style saviour. A versatile item that will take you from a day full of meetings to post-work cocktails in elegant ease, you should have one in your wardrobe at all times. Victoria Beckham, Roksanda, Stella McCartney and Roland Mouret are all brilliant brands to look at to fulfil the need. A block colour or two-tone design will work best. Cleverly chosen accessories, such as a bold cuff, statement shoe or smart clutch will bring the required glamour. If the event is in the country rather than the city, you can loosen up slightly by choosing a print or a softer silhouette, perhaps a fluted hem or draped blazer, rather than sharp tailoring. Think dressed-up daywear without the restrictions of morning dress.

DESTINATION BEACH

Beach weddings may be held in a place where you usually wear as little clothing as you can get away with, but they are still a serious event. It shouldn't look as though you were sunbathing and then just wandered up the aisle. Make sure your outfit is practical – it's going to be hot, hopefully, so light, dreamy fabrics and non-clingy shapes are key – but kaftan details and see-through fabrics are absolute no-nos. Look for something that is a little fancier than a normal wedding dress to make it clear you are here for the party. Likewise, your shoes need to not sink in the sand, but anything flip-flop inspired looks inelegant; try a wedge. Wearing something in your hair, even just a jewelled clip or comb, will make it feel like an occasion outfit rather than a day in the sun.

SMART CASUAL

It's the most derided dress code of all for its contradictory direction. For the love of God, which is it? Do you want us smart *or* casual? In fact, it's one of the easiest to interpret because it allows your own fashion sense in, whereas some of the other dress codes are so rigid they obliterate all personal taste. Right now, an embellished sweatshirt and pencil skirt combo or leather leggings with a tailored blazer would be the on-trend interpretations of the code. If you're still in doubt, look at the way French *Vogue* editor Emmanuelle Alt dresses during Paris Fashion Week. She always looks immaculate but never overdressed, which is fashion anathema as well as the biggest smart-casual sin. Perfectly fitted jeans, a double-breasted blazer and slouchy linen T-shirt are her uniform, worn with a panache that only the French seem to be able to pull off, but which you can, too. Add a flash of metallic from shoes you can walk in, but make sure they're shoes rather than trainers, as these will bring the outfit into the perfect smart-casual balance, whereas trainers are too informal and will tip it into casual-casual territory. Add a roomy daytime clutch (nothing too embellished) rather than a daytime satchel (too casual). Your colour palette can be dictated by what suits you and where you're headed, but if anything feels too office-y it's too smart, so ditch it. This dress code can send some people the wrong direction style-wise, so be prepared that some guests might look as though they're off to do the supermarket shop. To counteract the overly casual attendees, make sure your outfit looks great without the jacket so you can dial down the smartness if you wish. Or leave it on and shame them for looking so damn scruffy!

COCKTAIL DRESS

An American term for evening wear that is fancy, fun and made for dancing. It shouldn't be a day-to-night style, but something you would only wear for special night-time shenanigans. Go for beading and embellishment if your dress is short but pick a plain style if you're going longer: embellishment will make a floor-length dress too gown-like and black-tie appropriate. Knee-length is best, and add a jacket you can shoulder-robe and shoes you can dance in. This dress code is less traditional, so the hosts are likely to appreciate outfits that are more fashion-forward and edgy. Jewel tones, leopard print and rich detailing will all be the perfect mix.

WEDDING OUTFIT ISSUES

If you don't like floral dresses it might seem that wedding season holds a barrage of problems and etiquette questions, but don't fret. This is what you need to know to answer the most common dilemmas.

1 What if I don't do dresses?
And? This, the least problematic wedding-guest outfit dilemma ever, barely warrants the question. Spend your time instead worrying about how to avoid weird Uncle Frank, or what on earth to choose from the gift list... A dress is the one-stop solution to most occasion dressing, but it is certainly not the only answer. A trouser suit looks suitably formal and if you choose a strong print or floral pattern it's easily fun enough for a celebratory day. A combination of pale lace blouse and silver pleated midi skirt or wide-leg trousers would be a clever mix of separates, while a jumpsuit offers the same just-one-piece ease of a dress while being far more fresh and modern, and much less prissy than a frock.

2 Can I wear black to a wedding?
Goths get married too, you know. Of *course* you can wear black. It all depends on the shape, silhouette, accessories, venue and time of year. Add a Morticia Addams veil to a black velvet floor-length dress in June and it would look creepy, but team a strapless puffball dress with a gold bag and metallic heel and wear it to a December wedding in a castle and it will look soigné and sophisticated. A wide splash of violet-coloured velvet ribbon around your waist and flowers in your hair will make you look like an extra from a Dolce & Gabbana ad campaign, which is a good thing. A raven on your shoulder is not. Black is particularly chic at evening and city weddings and winter events in general. A sharp trouser suit in jet black is an elegant option and, as well as metallics, also looks great with white and pastels. The only time I would avoid a black dress would be for a morning country church ceremony in mid-summer, although even then you could choose a black-based floral (inspired by Céline or Balenciaga) or wear it in moderation, perhaps choosing black lace to break up the weight of the fabric.

3 And what about white?
The thing about wearing white to a wedding is: why on earth would you want to? I realize that black is a comfort colour, so the above is a valid question. But white most certainly isn't an easy shade to wear. It's unlikely to be the only colour that suits you and, while it does look good with a tan, it's rather unnecessary to base your outfit and incite the bride's ever-lasting dismay because you looked better on Her Special Day. Colours are subjective, and the bride herself is as likely to be in ivory or buttermilk as pure white, but wearing any white-ish tones to a wedding will make you look like a bunny boiler, however innocent your intentions. If you must wear white on pain of death, choose a high-necked silk blouse and wear it with a pastel-toned tweed skirt suit to dial down the drama that a white dress would cause.

4 I don't want to buy something I'll only wear once.
Quite right. There is enough fashion wastage in the world. My preference would be for a silky T-shirt, perhaps with panels of printed brocade, a jewelled neckline or a lace collar. It will look brilliant with a full skirt or slim-leg trousers and a blazer, or under a lightweight coat at the wedding, but you will also be able to get mileage out of it by teaming it with a statement skirt for a dressy event, slipping it under a suit for evenings out with work colleagues, or layering it with a cardigan and jeans for a cosy pub date. A statement skirt would also be a versatile choice, but these sort of skirts need plainer top halves to shine. Other guests will see more of your top half when sitting in the ceremony and at dinner, so it's wiser to choose a flashy top rather than bottom.

5 I've several weddings this year where I'll see the same group of people.
This is a tricky issue, and one that can't be solved simply by wearing the same dress with different accessories, or by getting those people so drunk they won't remember what you wore. It's questions like this that make me wish I had paid more attention in maths instead of doodling shoes on my workbooks. If you have three weddings to go to you could buy one slip dress and two tops. At wedding one, wear the dress under top one (belt it all in, if necessary); at wedding two, wear the dress alone; at wedding three, wear the other top *under* the dress. Alternatively, you could choose one statement skirt and mix it with a different top each time. As I mentioned above, people will focus on your top half more, so the bottom half of your outfit can be more anonymous. More than three weddings? You will need to choose some different friends or add one other dress to my first suggestion; then you'll get two more outfit options, taking your total number of wedding looks up to five.

6 What on earth should I wear on my head?
Don't panic. You don't *have* to wear a hat – although a friend told me about a wedding she was invited to that had a 'strictly no hats' policy, which she was distraught about. A no-hat policy is as dictatorial as being told your hem must cover your knees so, in the spirit of fashion being fun, if you want to wear a hat to a wedding, you should. But if the thought panics you, calm down. Just remember that fascinators are fashion anathema. Jewelled clips, pearl-embellished combs and wide grosgrain-ribbon headbands with mini veils are far more acceptable if you're hat-phobic. What is appropriate absolutely depends on where the wedding is and when. A faux-fur cossack hat will look perfect for a winter wedding, a festival-style floral crown will look great at a summer vineyard wedding in rural France. The point of a hat, and of headwear in general, is to show you've made an effort for the wedding, and that you're not just turning up in 'this old thing'.

A YEAR

IN

FASHION

JANUARY

Following the festive binge, this month is the perfect time to avoid the shops and try out a shopping ban to help you truly understand what your wardrobe needs for the year ahead. Dark, cold days are ideal for staying in and having a wardrobe clear-out to work out what you'll actually wear this year, and what gaps you might need to fill.

FEBRUARY

This is American awards season, when Hollywood's A-Listers provide plenty of inspiration for event dressing on the red carpet of the Grammys, the Golden Globes and the Oscars. Take note: the big star's gowns will influence next year's wedding dress trends, too.

MARCH

The international autumn collections are revealed to fashion press and buyers on the catwalk at presentations in New York, London, Milan and Paris.

APRIL

The Costume Institute Gala, otherwise known as the Met Ball or, less formally, Fashion's Oscars, falls at the end of the month or the very start of May. A fundraising event for New York's Metropolitan Museum of Art's Costume Institute, the gala's theme and dress code coincides with the gallery's current exhibition and attracts every major name in fashion, music and film, and often influences the next season's trends.

MAY

This is when the biggest fashion houses show their Cruise or Resort collections. Originally designed for well-to-do society women needing lighter clothes for their winter sun travels (literally, cruising), now the catwalk shows appear wherever in the world that takes a fashion house's fancy: California, Texas, Kyoto, Blenheim Palace, Rio...

JUNE

Don't leave buying your holiday wardrobe too late. Shop for swimwear and summer dresses at the start of the month.

JULY

The sales season is in full swing. It's so easy to get caught up in the rush, so only venture in if you have strong resolve and a shopping list. Always check the store's returns policy on sales items before you hand over your cash.

AUGUST

All the main autumn drops will start to filter in store. It might feel odd if the weather is hot, but this is when you should buy your winter coat.

SEPTEMBER

The international catwalk collections for spring of the following year are shown in New York, London, Milan and Paris and the glossy magazines' biggest issues of the year hit the newsstands.

OCTOBER

As the seasons change it's the ideal time to reassess your wardrobe. Clean and pack away any summer clothes and switch over your wardrobe to cold-weather essentials.

NOVEMBER

This is when Cruise collections arrive in store and they will stay full price (and not go on sale) until next year's Summer sales. If you fancy a pre-new season pick-me-up that hints at next year's trends, they are an ideal place to find a treat.

DECEMBER

Party season calls for clever clothes you can style in lots of different ways to avoid buying a new dress for every event. Shop carefully and cleverly.

DIRECTORY

BRAND DIRECTORY

This is certainly not an exhaustive list of every store on the high street, but they are the brands that have created a niche for themselves and the ones that I turn to again and again for everything, from new-season refreshers to classic pieces. My definition of high street is that they have a standalone store out of London (so aren't just a one off boutique you'll only find in the capital) or are an online business that will ship nationwide.

& Other Stories
www.stories.com
Divided into collections designed in LA, Paris and Stockholm, everything in Stories feels more considered and detailed than classic high-street fare, even the minimal pieces.

ASOS
www.asos.com
Their own-label offering is vast and covers every trend of the season for every body shape and style. Always filter by brand and size in order not to be overwhelmed by scrolling.

Boden
www.boden.co.uk
There are *a lot* of prints and patterns on the site, but search for the cashmere – always super soft, in a brilliant array of colours – and the shoes, which are playful and fun.

COS
www.cosstores.com
If one of your three words is minimal and pared-back style is your signature, COS will be the store for you. The subtle palette of neutral shades is perfect for creative office workwear.

Debenhams

www.debenhams.com

The first high-street store to introduce designer collaborations, Studio by Preen and H by Henry Holland are the style set's two current favourites.

Finery

www.finerylondon.com

A new online-only store, Finery's designs offer a little bit extra compared to regular high-street buys and they are particularly strong on midi-length and long-line dresses.

French Connection

www.frenchconnection.com

Every season, French Connection will nail the trends with a selection of spot-on, trend-led pieces that will sell out. Quality is paramount.

Gap

www.gap.com

It's not the most exciting brand on the block, but Gap remains my go-to for casual, preppy essentials. Stock up on well-made tees and hoodies to work the high–low mix with some of your fancier finds.

H&M

www.hm.com

Their annual collaborations with major designer names are legendary – Erdem, Isabel Marant, Marni, Stella McCartney, Alexander Wang – while the year-round Studio collection offers fast fashion fixes.

John Lewis

www.johnlewis.com

Not the first store that comes to mind for fashion, John Lewis's Modern Rarity collection is an insider secret with classic designs from some of London's coolest names – Eudon Choi and Palmer // Harding.

Kitri

www.kitristudio.com

Uploading a small selection of new pieces every week, online-only store Kitri offers a fresh take on trends while not stinting on quality (yet still keeping prices realistic).

Next

www.next.co.uk

Getting more trend-led every season, the shoes are particularly desirable. Now there is the Label/Mix capsule collection with an edgier, fashion-led offering, too.

Marks & Spencer

www.marksandspencer.com

So much more than brilliant bras and knickers, M&S does fantastic cashmere. There are several lines in store: Collection elevates everyday essentials, Autograph is all about sleek classics and Limited is the youngest, most fun line.

Mango

www.mango.com

Mango has had a recent design reboot and their signature style has become much more trend-led. Their earrings are a firm fashion favourite, as is their huge denim collection.

River Island

www.riverisland.com

For fast, affordable buys – and the ultimate Friday night outfit – River Island can't be beaten. Their denim is stand-out, as is the chunky knitwear, which has more longevity than other high-street knits I've worn.

Topshop

www.topshop.com

The giant of the high street has its own catwalk slot at London Fashion Week. If you're looking for clothes, shoes, bags, jewellery or accessories, Topshop's website or massive Oxford Circus store will have it, and they offer an edited selection of independent brands, too.

Uniqlo

www.uniqlo.com

A quiet force focusing on the basics, the Heattech range is every stylist's secret weapon when shooting in cold locations, and the merino and cashmere knits are brilliant value. Look out for the occasional collaborations with fashion insiders such as Carine Roitfeld, Inès de la Fressange and JW Anderson.

Warehouse

www.warehouse.co.uk

With a recent revamp under design director Emma Cook, there are lots of prints made to clash, texture contrast and a very British playfulness. All the trends are in store, as well as plenty of cool classics.

Whistles

www.whistles.com

Certainly at the expensive end of the high street – the sheepskin coats veer into four figures – Whistles is cleverly designed without being too quirky and is a great place for office outfits and occasion dressing.

Zara

www.zara.com

Openly inspired by catwalk trends and key designer pieces. Whether you're into bold Balenciaga statements, chic Céline style or a Gucci-esque eclectic mix, Zara has it all, at prices you can afford to experiment with.

THE NEW NAMES TO KNOW

A few choice gems from any of the brands below will elevate your outfits to a new level. These are the labels that women in their home countries rely on, and which are emerging elsewhere, too.

Storets
www.storets.com
A US brand that ships worldwide for free (on orders over 75). The pieces are beyond basic with lace trims, cut-outs and off-the-shoulder details aplenty.

Sandro
fr.sandro-paris.com

Maje
uk.maje.com
Individually created by two sisters, it's unsurprising that Maje and Sandro share a similar DNA. You'll find all the classics with an ultra-desirable, French-girl twist at both stores.

Ganni
www.ganni.com
This Danish label is designed by a team of creatives and has become a favourite with the fashion pack for their mohair sweaters and cult fruit motif T-shirts.

J Crew
www.jcrew.com
Featuring a stellar collection of all-American classics, J Crew can look incredibly preppy when worn together, but mix it up with an eclectic sensibility and it looks arty and perfectly styled.

ONLINE

These are my top five designer department stores, the one-click wonders that have a collection of the hottest catwalk looks, must-have basics and undiscovered brands. Buyers are just as influential as stylists in creating the mood of the season, and these stores have the best edits and are the sites – and apps – I check religiously for everything from essential underwear to statement jewels.

Matches Fashion
www.matchesfashion.com

Style Bop
www.stylebop.com

Farfetch
www.farfetch.com

Net-A-Porter
www.net-a-porter.com

Browns Fashion
www.brownsfashion.com

SECOND HAND

These choice shops offer a mix of buys from the most exquisite vintage couture gowns through to unique-but-affordable fixes. They're the top spots for some second-hand chic.

Rellik
www.relliklondon.co.uk
Where Kate Moss gets her original Vivienne Westwood pirate boots, Rellik's rails are full of significant fashion pieces and a careful curation of important vintage items.

Beyond Retro
www.beyondretro.com
From a vast warehouse in east London – with other stores around the capital, Brighton and in Sweden – Beyond Retro is as close to a chain store as vintage can be. Sifting out retro gems, they steer close to mainstream trends for a seasonally relevant edit.

Kerry Taylor Auctions
www.kerrytaylorauctions.com
Probably the most knowledgeable woman in Britain on the subject of vintage clothing, Kerry's auctions showcase a mix of costume and private collections of the most jaw-dropping fashion discoveries. Go here to dream about lives lived in exquisite style.

Vintage Modes
Housed inside Grays Antique Centre, along with dozens of antique dealers, Vintage Modes is a collective of expert stalls specializing in art deco jewellery, silks and clothes that often find their way onto photoshoots for *Vogue*.

William Vintage
If an actress on the red carpet is wearing vintage, it's likely to be from William Banks-Blaney's W1 boutique. With a huge collection of immaculate couture pieces, everything is ozone treated (to remove lurking smells and spores) to make this as far away from the musty vintage shopping experience as you can imagine.

OUTLET

How to bring personality to your wardrobe? Shop off from the beaten track. Search out past-season gems and track down the ones that got away at any of these outlet and resale sites.

Bicester Village
www.bicestervillage.com
With boutiques just like the ones on Bond Street, but selling pieces at up to 90 per cent off, Bicester is my happy place. It's like an extra-long village street with cute clapboard stores and the biggest Pret A Manger in Britain. I can't get by without at least one trip a year; Balenciaga, Céline and Saint Laurent are my current favourite shops. It's easy to see why Bicester is the UK's second biggest tourist attraction after Buckingham Palace. Get there as early as you can and aim to be away by midday – and never, ever visit on the weekend.

Depop
www.depop.com
The mobile store and app is a favourite with bloggers for selling their gently worn outfits, but you can discover vintage finds and home decor too.

Etsy
www.etsy.com
Independent brands sell their designs in a crafty environment. Particularly good for unusual jewellery or finding an individual slogan T-shirt.

Hardly Ever Worn It
www.hardlyeverwornit.com
Selling luxury brands, this resale site has a whole category devoted to celebrity and VIP sellers.

The Outnet
www.theoutnet.com
A sister brand of net-a-porter.com, you'll find out-of-season designer buys and own label Iris & Ink, which is great for wardrobe-filling essentials. Drops happen on Monday, Tuesday and Thursday mornings, plus there are occasional flash sales with huge discounts up for grabs.

Tictail
www.tictail.com
An independent marketplace that offers a space for emerging designers to sell their wares online.

Vestiaire Collective
www.vestiairecollective.com
Where to search for The One That Got Away. Set an alert for pieces that you missed first time round and if they are listed on this designer resale site, perhaps you'll get lucky next time. The French-founded site sells for French *Vogue* editors and many fashion insiders.

WARDROBE CARE

All the gear and no idea? Store your shoes, bags and clothes right and you'll look polished on every occasion. Every stylist's secret address book will hold these names.

The Restory
www.the-restory.com
When your bags and shoes are looking a little lacklustre, this company will restore their life.

Elias
www.eliascleaners.co.uk
Offering dry-cleaning to beyond immaculate standards, Elias also do bag repairs and restorations.

Valentinos
www.valentinodrycleaners.com
They used to do twice-weekly pick-ups at Vogue House, will take up trousers and can dry-clean almost any stain. Take cash – you may need to pay in advance for leather or suede cleaning – and don't baulk at the prices. Alexander McQueen send all their samples there. It's worth it.

Morplan
www.morplan.com

For hangers, rails and clothes storage, the Morplan catalogue is a dream read for anyone with a yen to get organized. Stock up on supplies that will keep your closet immaculate.

Amazon
www.amazon.co.uk

A brilliant source for storage boxes, shelf dividers, hooks and non-slip hangers.

John Lewis
www.johnlewis.com

Shop for hangers, lavender bags and that wardrobe essential, the handheld steamer.

INSTAGRAM INSPIRATION

If you find yourself in a style rut, a browse on Instagram's fashion-insider feeds will give you more ideas to restyle your wardrobe than a shopping trip ever could. These are my favourite names to follow.

Linda Rodin
@lindaandwinks

The former stylist and founder of Rodin skincare proves that age is no barrier to looking chic and prefers to thrift her colourful wardrobe than spend a fortune in designer boutiques.

Caroline Issa
@carolineissa

As fashion director of *Tank* and *Because* magazines, Caroline has access to all the trends but distills them perfectly to match her own elegant and modest style.

JJ Martin
@jjmartinmilan

An American in Italy and editor-at-large of *Wallpaper** magazine, JJ's feed is a masterclass in how to clash prints with panache.

Miroslava Duma
@miraduma

The petite Russian is a business powerhouse, launching websites and fashion tech start-ups as her day job – but she also shows that being just over five feet tall shouldn't stop you experimenting with volume.

Tamu McPherson
@tamumcpherson

Street-style photographer and founder of the blog alltheprettybirds.com, Tamu mixes statement pieces, ruffles and prints with streetwear and jeans, perfectly exemplifying the High–Low mix.

INDEX

THANK YOU

With huge gratitude to my editor at Pavilion, Stephanie Milner, for her patience and guidance. If Stephanie hadn't spotted me on the street and had faith in my ability to write a book (which I didn't share), you would not be reading this today. Also, huge thanks to the rest of the team who worked on this book, especially Laura Russell for her visionary design and illustrator Bijou Karman – I can't believe someone as cool as Bijou was part of this project and her clever illustrations have given life to my words.

Likewise, if my wonderful mother Christine had not instilled a love of shoes, clothes and shopping in me by inspiring me with her own incredible personal style, I would have nothing to write about. Thank you mummy. And if I hadn't inherited my charming father's journalistic talent and grammatical expertise, I wouldn't be able to write it with any sense of eloquence. Thank you, daddy.

Last but no means least, thank you to my husband Colum. The kindest, most supportive, loving, handsome and stylish man I know, he has put up with me and my wardrobe for the past seventeen years and deserves more than an acknowledgement in this book as his reward. A knighthood for services to shopaholics or a medal would be more appropriate. Thank you, darling.

ABOUT THE AUTHOR